PREFACE

I had achieved the American dream: a house, a car, a steady job, and even a loving family. I traveled for my employer and saved money so that one day, I could see the rest of the world. My life was going according to plan, yet I felt unfulfilled. I realized that the upkeep of this traditional lifestyle was sucking my time and energy. I felt overwhelmed by the perpetual chores and errands, and by the long workdays and commute. A shift in my awareness allowed me to embrace a new joyful lifestyle where I began focusing on my life priorities: love, freedom, exploring, and having fun!

At age 35, I chose to eliminate 95% of my belongings and travel the world by living in hotels. My personal belongings fit in two suitcases. My space, as well as my mind, are now clutter-free, and I have time to focus on what is truly important.

Surprisingly, I found that living in hotels is LESS expensive than owning or renting a home. I spend less money enjoying a service-based hotel residence than I did as a homeowner, where I spent money on furniture, appliances, stuff, stuff to hold the stuff, utility bills, property insurance, fees, and home maintenance. Hotels provide for all my basic needs, and I pay as I go.

For most of the past decade, I have worked remotely – most often from my hotel room, a cruise ship, a café, or a poolside. I have lived in over 100 cities across the U.S., UK, Canada, the Netherlands, Germany, Switzerland, and Panamá. I have visited many other countries as well, tasted a variety of amazing food, and gained new friends from a variety of cultures. Among the many wonderful meaningful benefits, a nomadic lifestyle has given me a broader perspective and an appreciation for diversity.

Although I work full-time, I feel like I'm on vacation every day of my life. Hotel living keeps me comfortable, safe, relaxed, and even pampered. I have no chores or errands. Housekeeping keeps my room tidy, and maintenance takes care of any issues. Hotels provide access to a swimming pool, hot tub, gym, and business center. Loyalty returns additional benefits like free nights, free food, suite upgrades, and access to elite club lounges.

Hotel Sweet Home shares what it's like to be a hotel-dwelling digital nomad. I describe the notable benefits and experiences, as well as how I've addressed challenges. I even provide a detailed cost comparison between living in hotels, renting a home, and owning a home.

I also share my best tips and insider secrets for anyone who visits hotels. I show how affordable hotel rooms can be using promotions, credit cards, and points. Travelers and nomads alike will appreciate the handy tips and reference guides for booking, checking in and out, and eating in hotel rooms. Frequent travelers will learn the most effective ways to use loyalty points for benefits like complimentary food, gifts, free nights, and suite upgrades.

Whether you stay in hotels or are just curious about a minimalist, hotel-living lifestyle, I hope you'll find Hotel Sweet Home interesting and useful.

Hotel Sweet Home

2021 Edition

by Libby Rome

Copyright © 2021 Libby Rome

Cover illustration by Theresa Johnson, https://www.theresajohnson.com

All rights reserved. No part of this publication may be reproduced, stored in a retrieval system, or transmitted in any form or by any means, electronic, mechanical, recording or otherwise, without the prior written permission of the author.

First Edition published 2019

DISCLAIMER: This book details the author's personal experiences with and opinions about living in hotels and minimalism. The author is not licensed as an educational consultant, teacher, psychologist, or psychiatrist.

The author is providing this book and its contents on an "as is" basis and makes no representations or warranties of any kind concerning this book or its contents. The author disclaims all such representations and warranties, including for example warranties of merchantability and educational or medical advice for a particular purpose. Also, the author does not represent or warrant that the information accessible via this book is accurate, complete, or current.

Except as specifically stated in this book, neither the author or publisher, nor any authors, contributors, or other representatives will be liable for damages arising out of or in connection with the use of this book. This is a comprehensive limitation of liability that applies to all damages of any kind, including (without limitation) compensatory; direct, indirect or consequential damages; loss of data, income or profit; loss of or damage to property and claims of third parties.

WHAT IS IT LIKE TO LIVE IN HOTELS?

Hotel living replaces chores and errands with time to read, walk, breathe, think, exercise, and play! However, some of the downsides are quite significant. As someone who has lived in hotels for most of the past decade, I share my perspective on the primary benefits and the challenges.

Twenty Awesome Benefits of Hotel Living

1. No chores

Hotel living means I no longer have to dust, sweep, mop, vacuum, make the bed, take out the garbage, clean toilets, or wash dishes. Even during the pandemic, I can contact housekeeping services anytime to clean my room. I also don't need to worry about repairing anything. If my air conditioning doesn't work well, or if my toilet overflows at 2 a.m., I call maintenance. They fix the issue quickly, or hotel management accommodates me, sometimes by upgrading me to a better room.

2. No errands

I no longer spend my evenings and weekends running one errand after another. I am glad to be rid of the driving, parking, shopping, standing in lines, and dealing with returns and exchanges.

I still may need to go to a doctor's appointment or buy something now and then, but those kinds of events now seem less like errands, and more like occasional activities that keep me healthy, comfortable, and happy.

3. No bills to pay

I pay no utilities, property insurance, nor property taxes. I no longer sit on the phone with utility and service companies. My hotel room includes utilities like water, electric, gas, Internet, and cable TV with movie channels.

I use automatic payments on my credit cards to systematically pay my hotel bills. The hotel e-mails me a copy of the receipt, and I could use the hotel and credit card apps on my iPad to view the transactions. I'm fortunate not to live paycheck to paycheck, and hotel living has few financial surprises. Therefore, I have a consistent peace of mind regarding my finances.

4. No clutter

Instead of owning things, I have a service-based lifestyle. If I want to cook, I rent a hotel room that has a kitchen and kitchen supplies. If I want to go skiing, I rent ski equipment. If I want to look great for a week of work meetings, I rent professional clothes online.

Having a tidy environment keeps my mind clutter-free. It's peaceful to know that everything is in its place, and there are no piles of paperwork or junk collecting dust. I feel less stressed, and I can focus better on my work and play.

5. More free time

Because I don't run errands and do chores, I can focus on my priorities. Life is short, and I much prefer to use my precious time for travel, to enjoy nature, to help loved ones, to improve myself, and to write this book!

6. Fun

I have always considered staying in hotels as fun and adventurous. I'm happy to report that that feeling hasn't changed, even after sleeping in hotels for thousands of nights. I have fun checking out a new hotel, and I have fun at the pool and hot tub. Some hotels offer happy hour or access to a lounge with complimentary food for elite guests.

Even the process of finding my next hotel is exciting. Others may fear not knowing what the future holds, but I enjoy the freedom of choosing my destinations and changing my plans as I see fit. I wake up excited about where I am every day.

7. Comfort

Premium hotels ensure a certain comfort level. I can rely on quality, comfortable beds and pillows to ensure a good night's sleep. My husband and I enjoy lounging in the common areas, sometimes with a book or a board game by the fireplace. Club lounges offer added comfort.

I can request anything to help ensure my stay is comfortable. For example, when the hotel water temperature is too low, I ask that maintenance turn it higher. When I first check into my room, I make sure the mattress and pillows are comfortable. If for some reason they're not, housekeeping sets up a new mattress or moves me to a different room.

Marriott-branded hotels offer services through their Marriott Bonvoy app. Guests can use the app to easily order housekeeping services or amenities, like a robe, slippers, and extra towels. When I prefer privacy, I place a "Do Not Disturb" sign on my door. If I don't feel completely comfortable, I could choose to move to a different hotel.

8. Access to facilities

I enjoy having a swimming pool and hot tub without the hassle of maintaining them. The hotel gym is convenient with at least some treadmills, stationary bikes, and free weights. There are no membership costs, and showers are right upstairs in the privacy of my own room.

I can get change, buy stamps, and mail letters from the front desk or hotel convenience store. Most hotels also have a guest laundry room with at least one coin-operated washing machine and dryer. They also offer a business center with computers and printers, and most office supplies are available for free upon request.

9. Being pampered

Upon my arrival at a new hotel, an attendant greets me and helps with my bags. The check-in process is usually friendly and welcoming, especially when I'm a return guest. With the highest loyalty elite status, I enjoy priority service, early check-in and late check-out, and the best complimentary upgrades. I proceed to my new room feeling spoiled with attention.

Premium hotels like the Hilton have a "Make it Right" policy that guarantees my satisfaction with every stay. If the hotel cannot address an issue, they usually compensate with free nights, food and drink vouchers, spa treatments, points, or other gifts.

Living in premium hotels means I benefit from many indulgent services. When I was in a taxi accident in Frankfurt, Germany, my hotel, the Marriott Frankfurt, called a doctor to see me in the executive lounge. He diagnosed me, wrapped up my sprained arm, and gave me a prescription. Hotel staff then filled and brought my prescription to me in my room. My total bill for the doctor's visit and medicine was less than $100. There was no charge for the excellent, caring personal service by the hotel.

10. Loyalty rewards

Major hotel chains, like Marriott, Hilton, and Hyatt, offer loyalty programs. Once you register as a member, you earn a higher status the more you stay. The highest loyalty status provides the following benefits at most hotels:

- An average of 20% of my spending returned as points toward free nights
- Complimentary upgrades
- Complimentary breakfast or food credit
- Club or executive lounge access (with more complimentary food)

- Early check-in and late check-out
- Suite nights (guaranteed complimentary suite upgrades)
- Priority service (e.g., separate check-in line with a red carpet)
- More amenities, like bottled water, snacks, a refrigerator, and a microwave

One of my favorite rewards is receiving an upgraded room or suite. When I book the least expensive, standard room, the hotel upgrades me to a more spacious room or a suite on the top floors with the best views. For example, the Sheraton Sand Key Resort in Clearwater, Florida, upgraded my room to a large, top-floor junior suite overlooking the ocean. I had access to complimentary food and drinks (including alcohol) in the lounge throughout the day.

11. Easy commute

I choose hotels that are within walking distance to the places I want to go, including my workplace. There is no need to sit in traffic or use the underfunded, overcrowded U.S. mass transportation system. The fresh air and sunshine improve my health and my outlook while I enjoy quality time to reflect or to converse with my husband.

Many hotels offer a complimentary hotel shuttle within a five-mile radius. You can use ride-sharing services Uber and Lyft for longer rides.

12. Free food and drinks

As the highest elite loyalty member, most of my hotel stays include a complimentary daily breakfast for two or vouchers for food and drinks. Many premium hotels also offer elite members access to a club lounge, also known as an executive lounge. Lounges usually offer breakfast, snacks throughout the day, and appetizers in the evening.

Hotel lounges abroad, and a few in the U.S., serve complimentary alcohol. For example, the lounge at the Sheraton Sand Key

Resort in Clearwater, Florida, serves wine and cocktails. Other hotels, like Marriott Residence Inn properties, offer a complimentary happy hour to all guests every evening.

13. Flexibility

Unlike rental agreements and homeownership, there are no entry and exit fees. I could live in hotels without any down payment or unexpected expenses. I could stop at any time and start again at any time.

If my hotel stay includes annoying neighbors, or if I don't like my hotel room, I could choose to move rooms or move hotels. If there are riots, a major storm approaching, or any other local issues, I could move to another city. If my income stopped or decreased, I could quickly decrease my expenses by moving to a less expensive hotel or location.

14. Variety

Living in hotels while working remotely provides an occasional change of scenery and the opportunity to experience an assortment of hotels and destinations. I leverage my minimalist lifestyle by simply grabbing my bags and heading off to wherever I feel like going next. Life is short, and I want to explore! After all, variety is the spice of life.

Sometimes I need nature, and sometimes I want to explore a new city. For example, I woke up one day and declared that I wanted to see monkeys in the wild; I was on a flight to Panamá, Central America later that day! Benefits of travel include experiencing new cultures, trying new food, meeting new people, and gaining new perspectives. My mind and my heart continue to grow as I explore.

15. No worries

When I owned a home, I would torment myself worrying: Did I leave the curling iron on? I could start a house fire! Did I forget to pay a bill? That could mean my utilities will turn off, my credit score gets hit, and I must pay extra fees.

There isn't much to worry about when it comes to hotel living. When I leave my hotel room, the hotel door locks behind me. If I accidentally break something in my hotel, someone else will fix it. I once ruined a range at a Holiday Inn Vacation Club hotel. I accidentally turned the heat on the stove burner with an empty pot sitting on it. The metal pan melted through the stove's glass top within minutes. I called downstairs to confess my destruction. Thirty minutes later, two maintenance men removed the old stove and replaced it with a new one. Despite having to carry those stoves up and down the stairs in 110-degree heat outside, they were even pleasant and laughing. I felt terrible, while also quite relieved and grateful!

16. Minimal stress

Life before hotel living includes constant worries, tedious chores, never-ending errands, growing clutter, and soul-crushing traffic. The stress made me grumpy, gain weight, and bicker with my loved ones. Hotel living eliminates the most stressful factors, so I stay calm and content. Hotel security, safety, comfort, and service give me peace of mind. Daily fun also sweeps away any potential stress from work or anything else. Both my mental and physical well-being have improved. For example, I no longer have high blood pressure!

17. Security

I guarantee a certain level of security by choosing premium-level hotels. I know I will have a well-secured room, usually with access to security personnel 24/7. Premium hotels comply with security standards like checking IDs every time someone asks for a replacement key, requiring a key to enter side doors and guest floors, and employing security cameras.

I have never experienced theft since living in hotels. If I did, I would move to a different hotel. I actively protect my work laptop, but the theft of my personal belongings would have a minimal impact. As a minimalist, I could re-purchase everything I need for less than $1,000. The Cloud stores and backs up my most valuable items, which are digital copies of photos, videos, and vital documents.

18. Safety

I don't compromise on safety, so if I don't feel safe in or around my hotel, I leave immediately. I typically do my research to avoid those situations, and hotel security always ensures I feel safe.

Hotels also have emergency response plans, with the ability to sound an alarm and notify guests upon a potential disaster. For example, a fire quickly surrounded my hotel in Agoura Hills, California, in the middle of the night in November 2018. Hotel staff knocked on every guest's door to evacuate guests. I quickly packed and said good-bye to my Penthouse suite at the Sheraton Agoura Hills, and an Uber driver took me to my next hotel in a nearby city. I hate to think what would have happened if my house, instead of my hotel, were surrounded by fire, and no one woke me up.

19. No pests

When I owned a home, I dealt with rats in my attic, ants eating everything in my pantry, silverfish throughout my kitchen, and spiders plaguing my daughter's bedroom. The last time I was in a vacation home, my husband woke up with a roach crawling on him. Hotel living means not having to worry about these pests.

I have encountered pests twice in my six years of hotel living. Once was a cockroach in a Florida hotel next to the water. The hotel sprayed my room, and I like to think any remaining cockroaches in the area found a better home than my room. I saw a mouse in my first-floor Amsterdam hotel room, which was directly above the Amstel Canal, next to the kitchen, and with sub-zero temperatures. The hotel manager moved me to a nicer room, delivered their best champagne and chocolate, and arranged a personalized Amsterdam tour as an apology.

Good housekeeping practices are the key to avoiding bed bugs, and premium hotels ensure their housekeeping staff attends the proper training. I can also check BedbugReports.com to see if anyone has reported bed bugs.

20. Minimal spending

Buying less means spending less. I no longer make impulse purchases. Before I buy something, I must feel confident that the purchase is a great value. Exploring local shops is less stressful when you have no intention or need to buy anything. I prefer to save my money, or to spend it on travel, experiences, and helping others.

Here is a bonus benefit! Did you know you can help fight trafficking by taking photos of your hotel room? It's yet another benefit of staying in hotels! TraffickCam is a database of hotel room images that investigators can use to find sexual perpetrators. It only takes a moment of your time, but it could save someone's life or well-being. Upload your hotel room photos at https://www.traffickcam.com. It's an easy way to give back and help others during your hotel stays.

Hotel Living Challenges

Hotel living has its challenges as well. Making friends is tough, and moving around can grow tiresome. Limited cooking options make it challenging to healthy and inexpensively. , Being in a small space with another person for extended periods takes some getting used to as well.

Hotels can also pose an additional risk for the spread of COVID-19 and other viruses. Even though hotels have ubiquitous signs about social distancing and wearing a maks, other guests don't often abide by the rules.

Another disadvantage to a nomadic minimalist lifestyle is the limitation of recreational activities. Certain hobbies are no longer feasible. For example, it's challenging to enjoy sports that require large or heavy equipment. You could rent equipment from sites like LowerGear.com, or you could purchase used items online. However, moving around still prohibits team and league experiences. You would need to consider travel-friendly and minimalist-friendly alternative activities, such as:

- Use technology to play online games, socialize, listen to music, and write.
- Use a small sketchpad and a set of graphite pencils to draw your ever-changing environment
- Work out in the hotel gym
- Go swimming
- Dabble in digital photography
- Take online singing lessons
- Take online yoga or exercise classes

The COVID-19 pandemic has left many of us lonelier than ever; most of us crave interacting with others. Moving around and staying in hotels does not generally help with that need. Being social is vital for growth and life satisfaction. Social media helps you stay in contact, but it's not the same. You can't give a shoulder to cry on, and you can't get to know friends' kids or take part in their life in a meaningful way. Remote working and limited hobbies also limit the number of people you meet, and it's hard to connect with someone on a deep level. On the bright side, the flexibility to travel enables you to visit friends and family, wherever they are.

Remote Working

The COVID-19 pandemic has been hard on all of us. However, it has also provided some positive changes. Companies have realized that they can save a lot of money and be even more effective by enabling their employees to work remotely.

A digital nomad is a person who moves around while working online. I also consider myself a global nomad (a "glomad") because I live a mobile and international lifestyle. I use telecommunication technology to work online from anywhere. A growing number of organizations, such as Amazon, Microsoft, and IBM, are increasingly implementing remote working. They pay less for facilities, and the employees appreciate the flexibility to take their kids to school or do chores throughout the day.

You can usually hook up your devices laptop to the hotel TV using an HDMI cable. You can also count on having a good Internet connection at hotels; but as a backup, consider a personal Wi-Fi (Mi-Fi) device that provides mobile high-speed Internet access. The Mi-Fi device is especially useful when you want to work on a beach, or anywhere else without a reliable and secure Internet connection. Instant messaging, online meetings, and e-mail enable remote workers to virtually collaborate with their teammates. You can also participate in many meetings using a smartphone.

Remote working has its pros and cons. It can be more challenging to establish strong relationships with others and to keep up with what's going on in the organization. However, the benefits can outweigh the cons. Remote working can enable employees to have higher productivity in a shorter amount of time while providing autonomy and flexibility. Remote workers don't need to spend time dressing up and commuting, so we have more precious time to ourselves.

Many people are working from home during the pandemic. However, as society opens back up, we may become increasingly more interested in community work environments, such as WeWork. They offer shared workspaces so you have a place to get your work done, and you can meet other professionals.

Life's Spice

Once the pandemic is over, your wanderlust may lead you to international travel. However, after many years of flying, I'm ready for Star Trek's transporters. Bean me up, please! Flying used to be fun, but it's mostly just a hassle getting through the lines and security, and airplane seats have become ridiculously cramped over the years. On the bright side, hotel loyalty elite status can often mean complimentary upgrades on United and Delta flights.

I love taking trains to get around Europe and along the U.S. coasts. Ride-sharing services are available in almost every country, so that makes it easy to get around. You can avoid stress from driving around a new city, and instead look out the window as someone else takes you door-to-door.

Physically moving from one location to another may be the most annoying and unpleasant part of hotel living. Even though I own very little, it still takes time to pack, commute, check in to a new hotel, unpack, and set up my laptop. Most moves require me to change my address on online delivery sites like Instacart on Amazon. If I'm staying for longer than a month, I may update my address with my employer and other institutions.

As the years have gone by, my husband Dan and I have both grown increasingly weary of constant travel. Moving around so much occupied a lot of my time and energy. I spent too much time thinking, "Where are we going to stay next?" and doing research and booking hotels to answer that question. I could hire an assistant to take over the research and booking, but that seemed indulgent, and I usually enjoyed the process when it didn't happen too much. Instead, we slowed down and started living in the same location for at least several months at a time. Another benefit of staying a while is that it helps to reduce travel and transportation expenses.

IS HOTEL LIVING RIGHT FOR YOU?

Hotel living provides a service-based, comfortable lifestyle with many benefits, like the flexibility to travel and move any time. It can even save you money. Best of all, it gives you FREEDOM and TIME. Life is an opportunity to experience our surroundings, learn and grow, relate to and help others, create art and ideas, and enjoy our loved ones. You'll finally have the time to spend on important activities like hobbies and being with family and friends.

If you're not fully confident that hotel living is for you, you can choose to ease into it. Take small steps. Instead of getting rid of your belongings, store them in a storage facility or at a family member's or friend's home. You could also rent your home while you move around. One of the benefits of hotel living is that you can always stop and return to your old lifestyle.

Candidates who might enjoy hotel living include:

Minimalists

Hotels supply almost everything you need to live comfortably: a secured room with furniture, a bathroom, amenities, and utilities. Most hotels also include cable TV, Wi-Fi, access to a pool, hot tub, gym, and business center. You don't need much more than some clothes. Hotel living encourages you to clearly define what you need vs. want. Inherent benefits ensue:

- Enjoy consistently clutter-free surroundings
- Save money

- Eliminate chores and errands
- Travel and move around easily
- Decrease your environmental footprint

Remote workers

Due to the pandemic, many large companies are transitioning from a traditional office environment to remote working. The employer often provides a laptop, smartphone, and telecommunications technology to collaborate with co-workers online. You can enjoy the flexibility of deciding when and where to work. For example, you can choose to rent out your home for half the year while you stay in a beach resort for the other half.

If you become a travelling remote worker, a.k.a., a "digital nomad," you can work from anywhere you want to be. If you're like me, no work-related situation can stress you out when you have the beautiful view and sounds of the ocean.

People who love travel

Hopefully, the COVID-19 pandemic will be over soon, and travel will be fully available to everyone again. Travel provides an amazing way to experience the world. It can expand your mind and give you a broader perspective and an appreciation of other cultures.

"To Travel is to Live" – Hans Christian Andersen

Hotel living gives you the ability to enjoy a variety of locations. Hotels exist in almost every country. As of 2021, Marriott properties span 131 countries and territories, Hilton properties span 119. Of course, the pandemic has greatly impacted our ability to travel, especially internationally. Hopefully, that will change and we'll be able to connect again.

Have you ever been on vacation, and wished that it wouldn't end? Hotel living allows you to stay as long as you desire, and to move along when you're ready for a new destination.

Do you want to:

- Be inspired?
- Enjoy an adventure?
- Experience other cultures?
- Eat a variety of food and cuisines?
- Gain a more global perspective?
- Learn and grow?
- Have the freedom to go where you want, when you want?
- Find your most ideal geographic location to eventually settle down?
- Find your international tribe?

The rich history, architecture, and breathtaking nature throughout this planet are moving. You will become wiser, stronger, and more enlightened due to the exposure to a variety of cultures, ideas, and perspectives.

People who travel for work

When the pandemic is over, at least some corporate travel will resume. If your employer is paying for your travel, hotel, and meals while you're at client sites and meetings, then why are you paying a mortgage or rent while you're on the road? With the money you save, you can stay in hotels, or wherever you want, in between your work travels.

If you're a consultant whose work travel takes you to the same destination every week, you can ask your employer to pay for a long-term hotel, rather than paying for your flights home on the weekend. Alternatively, you could travel to other destinations on weekends.

Recent or upcoming university graduates may especially find this lifestyle appealing if they will be traveling with their job. It's an opportunity to save money and see a variety of places before settling down.

People who prefer service over chores and errands

The reality of owning or renting a home involves constant

chores, errands, and frustrations. Hotel living accommodates your basic needs and provides above-and-beyond service. Housekeeping and maintenance take care of those tedious chores, and most of your errands no longer apply. The service-based, carefree lifestyle means you own your personal time.

People who like hotels

If you enjoy staying in hotels, the joy doesn't stop, even after years of living in them. The experience only gets better. You'll learn how to choose the best hotels and optimize your stays. Hotels also reward your loyalty with benefits like upgraded rooms, complimentary breakfast, and access to club lounges.

Every visit to a new hotel is an opportunity to experience something new. It's exhilarating to walk into a new grand lobby. They provide art and décor throughout the hotel, as well as a tidy room with an expertly made comfortable bed. It's also comforting to know that hotel staff is there 24/7 to accommodate your needs.

Teachers and seasonal employees

People who work only part of the year could enjoy the flexibility that hotel living provides. For example, teachers could live near their school nine months out of the year. With the loyalty points they'll earn, they could live free in a hotel at their preferred destination, like a beach or Paris, during the summers.

Young adults

Young people who haven't invested in belongings yet could leverage the opportunity to try out a variety of regions, rather than commit to maintaining a home and its contents. You could start your adult life expand your mind, and you may even find an ideal location to ultimately settle down in one day. If you don't move around, how will you know what you're missing?

Divorcees and Widows

Sometimes you need significant time away to collect yourself, for example, due to a divorce or death. It may be difficult or impossible to stay in your own home. Hotel living can be an effective life "reset button" because you're in a new environment where you could focus on healing and moving on. You could quit hotel life and settle down somewhere whenever you're ready.

Retirees

Living in hotels can be more enjoyable than living in potentially depressing retirement homes. Hotel staff will accommodate your basic needs, and you could enjoy replacing chores and errands with service. An increasing number of news articles have shared cases where retirees have found that living in a hotel is less expensive than retirement homes.

You could choose to enjoy your retirement moving around and traveling as you'd like. You may even find your ultimate retirement destination through travel. For example, you could stretch your money further by retiring in a country like Thailand or Panamá. You might be considering retirement living in Florida, but you want to try living a summer there to make sure you could tolerate the humidity. Hotel living lets you try a destination for a few months or years before committing.

Those who are Unemployed or Financially-challenged

People with debt and bad credit may find it challenging to get a mortgage or rent an apartment. There is no credit check to book a hotel room. There's also no first and last month's rent due, and there no need to sign up for utilities. Hotels typically supply cable TV, Internet access, unlimited hot water, and unlimited air conditioning. The service-focused hotel staff takes the place of an overbearing or unresponsive landlord. At the end of each stay, you could pay your hotel bill with a debit card, cash, or credit card.

If you declare bankruptcy, your credit rating will be low for six years, which may prevent you from buying a home or a car without a high-interest rate. You don't need those things with hotel living. Declaring bankruptcy also means you'll receive a plethora of (high interest) credit card offers. If you're able to pay off those credit card bills going forward, using them to pay your hotel bills improves your credit score.

Parents who want their children to see the world

Hotel living could be a great way to expose your child to a variety of places and cultures, while also demonstrating the ability to enjoy life with less stuff. Parents who work remotely and home-school their children are especially well suited.

Most hotels don't charge extra for children to stay in the room with you, plus breakfast is often free for kids. Families could enjoy the hotel pool and a change of scenery while seizing the opportunity to travel. If you'd like more intimacy, you can choose an all-suites hotel like Embassy Suites.

In-love couples

As the pandemic has taught us, continually being in close quarters with your partner can either be wonderful or awful. Hotel living requires a strong, honest, loving relationship with your partner. Not only are you in close quarters with them, but with no chores and errands, you end up spending even more hours with them every day. If that sounds appealing, then hotel living is ideal!

People who want to save money

Owning a home is a big commitment. After a large up-front investment, to make a home financially viable, you need to own it for many years. Hotel living can supply instant accommodations without that investment or need to buy furnishings.

Hotel living will also change your spending habits and can eliminate the continually compelling need to shop. It's easier to stay on budget when it only includes two items: your hotel bill and groceries. There are no surprises. Hotel living includes furniture, amenities, utilities, cable TV, Wi-Fi, pool, gym, business center, and housekeeping. After earning elite loyalty status, hotel living also includes perks that make it even more financially viable.

Also, if you travel often for work or pleasure, you're losing money if you're paying rent or a mortgage while you travel. If you live in hotels, the only cost for taking a vacation is transportation to the destination. Live where you explore!

Due to most hotel's central location, you may also no longer need a vehicle. You could walk to most of your destinations, like shops, grocery stores, and restaurants. Premium hotels often include a shuttle that drives you anywhere within a 5-mile radius. Instead, consider having a budget for ride-sharing services like Uber and Lyft. They are often less expensive than a car payment, parking fees, insurance, inspections, gas, and unpleasant surprises like break-downs and traffic tickets.

Seasonal tourists

Hotel living is great for following the weather. There is no need to own cold-weather clothes if you time your travels well. You could spend spring on a Caribbean Island, summer in Boston, fall in Amsterdam, and winter in Miami. You could change your destinations and durations as you see fit.

You can enjoy the Pacific Northwest in the summertime, the warmest season with the least rain; Portland and Seattle come alive with outdoor events and activities. My ideal winter destination is Tampa, Florida. I love the wildlife, water, people, food, and skylines in Tampa, but it's quite hot and humid in the summer.

People with health issues

Some people may benefit from living in a region with more affordable health care. Many medical procedures and medications cost significantly less in countries outside the U.S. For example, my friend with Type 1 diabetes must take an annual trip to Mexico to be able to afford her insulin.

Certain regions also have medical specialists. For example, the M.D. Anderson Cancer Center in Houston, Texas, is one of the leading cancer hospitals. I have met many Americans who lived in hotels abroad for alternative medical treatments. For example, I met one Hilton Panamá hotel guest who was visiting for several months while his wife received stem cell therapy.

People who work for large organizations or the government

Many organizations have hotel partnerships so that employees receive discounted rates. When you book a hotel room, you need to enter your corporate code. You could ask your employer's travel department for the corporate codes, or you could look up the organization at HotelCorporateCodes.com.

I have worked for large companies, especially the big consulting firms, most of my career. I use my employer's corporate code to get significantly lower prices than what the public sees. They help make hotel living affordable.

If you're friends with an employee of the hotels, the Friends and Family rate can provide some super affordable hotel living.

People who enjoy leveraging points

By leveraging credit cards, loyalty points, and promotions, staying in hotels can cost less than paying rent or a mortgage.

People who enjoy affordable locations

Finding an affordable hotel in big cities like New York, Boston, Los Angeles, or San Francisco is virtually impossible. Hotel costs vary greatly by location. Within the United States, rates are consistently high along the coasts but lower in the middle and southern regions. April and May are great months for affordable rates and pleasant weather in typically cold cities like Portland, Maine. Of course, hotel rates are lowest in countries with a lower cost of living. For example, you can find deals at decent hotels in Mexico and Thailand for less than $40/night.

EMBRACING MINIMALISM

Hotel living demands owning as little as possible. It's easy to clutter a small environment. Fortunately, hotels provide almost everything you need.

Hotel living includes a service-based lifestyle. Instead of owning and maintaining things, you can rely on hotels and other services to meet your needs. Ubiquitous online shops and service subscriptions, like Amazon and Instacart, easily replace most traditional shopping methods. Service subscriptions like Netflix, Hulu, and Amazon Prime provide a plethora of entertainment.

The Joys of Minimalism

Following are some of the benefits you'll enjoy becoming a minimalist:

Saving money

Eliminate bills, furniture, or endless spending on "stuff."

Freedom

Minimalism gives you freedom from continuously spending time and energy on material items. You can choose to spend time in a variety of other ways, and your mind is free to ponder ideas and create new thoughts.

No clutter

Without clutter, life has less chaos and fewer disruptions. Everything has its place, and you can quickly access what you need so it's easier to feel relaxed and calm.

Flexibility

Moving around and living in hotels is a lot easier with a light load. Being able to move around gives you the ability to try different places before you settle down. You also don't need to commit to a specific style or theme for your belongings – until you're ready to commit.

Adventure

You're ready for anything when you can pack all your belongings in 10 minutes!

Easy shopping

Grocery shopping is simpler and faster because there's no need to purchase household items, like toilet paper, tissues, and cleaning supplies. Clothes shopping is rare and can easily be done online these days.

Help others

There are millions of people who could use the myriad of home items that you're not using. Give away your belongings to a charity, such as United Way, or a local organization that helps the homeless or underprivileged.

Help the environment

Most people in Western society own too many things. It feels great to reduce consumerism and your environmental footprint.

Avoid the hassle of returns and exchanges

As more products became electronic and advanced, they also became outdated or useless more quickly. Many made-in-China products aren't made to last. For example, I owned two TVs that broke shortly after their one-year warranties ended, and I owned a vacuum cleaner that stopped working after only a month.

End the vicious cycle of spending

When you own things, you are easily compelled to buy more

things. For example, if you own a TV, you may want to buy a speaker system, a new DVD player, and a gaming console. Then you may "need" to buy DVDs, games, and better game controllers. When you buy a computer, you also require a mouse, mouse pad, keyboard, monitor, and printer. A printer requires a regular supply of ink cartridges and paper. Inevitably the electronic items broke, and you have to buy replacement parts. At some point, you may want to upgrade your computer with a better graphics card, more memory, more disk space, a better mouse, a new fun mouse pad, a better keyboard, a bigger monitor, a better printer, and better paper. An unrelenting desire to upgrade and improve your home and belongings is expensive and sucks up your time and energy.

Be a good role model

A minimalist lifestyle is great for children, too. They outgrow childhood toys and hobbies, and they can enjoy giving them away to other children who can use those items. Best of all, they're not starting life already in a cycle of endless consumerism.

Easily share memories

Storing your pictures and files electronically makes it significantly easier to organize, find, and share memories and information. For example, you could use a Cloud service like Microsoft OneNote to create shared albums with selected pictures you want your friends to see.

Minimize loss

Have you ever rummaged through your entire house, had the whole family looking for a lost item, wasting their time and as well as your own? Losing something is disruptive and stressful. Being a minimalist frees your mind and time.

Storing your files electronically also helps minimize loss. Electronic files stored in the cloud cannot be damaged or destroyed, by fire for example. You can also access them anytime from wherever you are in the world. Electronic files can easily be backed up to multiple locations as well, making it virtually impossible to lose your content.

Becoming a Minimalist

Different people have their own styles of minimalism. You can take it to a level that is comfortable for you. Do your possession control you? Do you want to gain back precious time and enjoy a clutter-free environment and mind? Consider the following tips to get started:

1. **Identify your needs vs wants**.

Do you own things you haven't looked at or used in over a year? Do you feel obligated to keep items of sentimental value or that were gifts? Can you eliminate redundant items? Consider storing these items in a separate space, or eliminating them altogether. Give away or throw away anything you haven't used in the past year.

2. **Take pictures**.

Is the item something you will enjoy looking at when you're older or sharing with others later? Take pictures of those items then eliminate them physically. Take pictures of your memorabilia, including childhood toys, collections, and even photo albums and scrapbooks.

In today's world, you don't need to keep physical records. Keep your passport, driver's license, and credit cards, and take photos of everything else. To minimize loss or damage, store your electronic files and pictures on cloud-based storage, like Apple iCloud, Microsoft OneDrive, and Google Drive, and Dropbox. You can look at them anytime you want to have a pleasant memory, and you can also share the images with others more easily.

3. **Take a long break from buying anything new**.

Do you really need more than one pair of jeans? Do you really need to upgrade your TV? Shop for clothes once or twice a year. Identify your style and favorite brands, and stick with them. Consider a policy that whenever you buy something new, you must eliminate something you already own.

4. Sell stuff.

Selling stuff is a hassle, but a few weekends of work can be rewarding – both financially and as a citizen. It can also help motivate you not to buy more stuff! You can sell items via garage sales and consignment shops, or you could sell online. It's time-consuming but critical to take pictures and write descriptions of your sell-able belongings. Consider your workplace's employee bulletin board. Other online options include:

eBay	http://www.ebay.com
Craigslist	http://www.craigslist.org
Kijiji (Canada)	https://www.kijiji.ca
Facebook Marketplace	http://www.facebook.com/marketplace

Finally, take time to feel the effects of having less stuff around you. Once you begin enjoying the benefits of minimalism, you'll likely never want to go back.

How Much Stuff Do you Need?

Due to the COVID-19 pandemic and the switch to remote working, many people have a wardrobe full of unwork work clothes. We've living primarily in our sweat pants these days, and things may not change much in the future given the likelihood of continued remote working.

Consider the following items as your basic set of personal items. Then ask yourself: *What else do I really need, and why?*

- 1 pair of pants
- 1 pair of shorts
- 3 shirts
- 1 pair of versatile, work-friendly sandals that fit well in

- a small space
- 1 scarf
- 1 light jacket
- 2 pairs of shoes
- 2 pairs of socks
- 1 bathing suit
- 5 pairs of undergarments
- Glasses and sunglasses
- 1 hat
- 1 bathroom kit containing a hairbrush, toothbrush, toothpaste, deodorant, razor, blunt scissors, tweezers, and nail clippers
- Medicine and medical supplies

Following are additional items that are handy when living in hotels:

- 1 collapsible measuring bowl – useful as a measuring cup and a handy bowl
- 1 paring knife to cut fruits and vegetables
- reusable bees wax paper to store leftovers
- 1 eye mask with earplugs for travel or as needed to sleep
- Small hobby supplies, such as a small sketchbook and graphite pencils

If you own an electronic device or computer, you may also consider owning:

- HDMI cable to use the hotel TV as a work monitor
- Headphones

You may also need to own medical equipment or supplies. As a person living with Type 1 diabetes, I often have months' worth of critical supplies. Fortunately, most major airlines, like Delta and United, allow an extra bag for medical needs. Consider purchasing a bag designated for your medical supplies.

Minimalism demands clothes that don't stand out. People pay attention to clothes that are wild, bright, or unique. I want to downplay that kind of attention, so they don't notice my tiny wardrobe rotation. I eliminated a large monthly dry-cleaning bill by slowly replacing most of my dresses with more sensible clothes.

You can use a service called Rent the Runway to rent up to four quality clothing items at a time. In the winter, you can rent a coat. When you need to look professional, simply choose your outfits online. After you're done wearing them, place the clothes back in their original container and dropped the package off at a UPS drop box. You can enjoy variety by choosing unique pieces that stand out – no one will ever see you in the same thing twice!

You may also consider giving up your car. Instead of driving, you use the free hotel shuttle service or enjoy the sun, fresh air, and health benefits of walking. Car-sharing services provide door-to-door pick-up and drop-off service often for less than owning and maintaining a car.

Owning a car comes with an endless to-do list, including paying for registration, buying insurance, regularly filling the gas tank, coordinating maintenance and inspections, finding and paying for parking, cleaning the car, and dealing with a traffic ticket or worse, a car accident. Cars are often just money pits, rich with chores and risks.

THE COSTS OF HOTEL LIVING

When I tell people I live in hotels, they often ask me if I'm rich. I am fortunate to have a stable job that pays well. However, living in hotels may be less expensive than you think. I live in premium hotels for an overall average of $100/night.

Most of the hotel living benefits still apply when choosing budget or mid-range hotels. They offer the same basic amenities as premium hotels but are a notch down on their décor, facilities, and services. I enjoyed a three-month stay at the Best Western Plus in Oregon City, Oregon, for $60/night. The rooms are clean and functional, with nice views, refrigerators, and large TVs with movie channels. Rates include daily breakfast at the attached restaurant, Riverside Bar & Grill, where the friendly service can't be beaten.

Hotel living offers many financial benefits, irrespective of most budgets. It can even be more affordable than owning a home or renting a home.

Financial Benefits

Following are financial benefits of hotel living:

Minimal spending

Buying a home has high transaction costs when buying and selling. It's also expensive to fill it with furniture, appliances, kitchen and bathroom supplies, cleaning supplies, and decorations. Buying things for your home can be fun at first, until the spending, cleaning, and reparations drain both your energy and your bank account. You may even agree with financial expert JL Collins's witty blog post: Why your house is a terrible investment. Renting also includes entry and exit fees, utilities, furnishings, and superfluous spending.

Hotel living encourages minimal spending. The hotel supplies complimentary soap, toothpaste, shampoo, cotton swabs, and razors. If I'm cold, the hotel brings me extra blankets or a space heater. I rarely buy anything other than a few groceries to supplement the complimentary hotel food.

Minimal debt

The American dream typically requires an unfortunate amount of debt. A mortgage, cars, and credit card balances make the average American poorer than a homeless person. Hotel living makes it easy to stay within your budget so that you can pay your credit card bills every month.

Minimal financial risk

Hotel living does not require homeowner's or renter's insurance, nor a security service. I have not experienced theft in my six years of hotel living. I no longer need to pay for home repairs, and I have never been liable after accidentally breaking things.

Flexibility

Hotel living enables moving around with little financial impact. If there's a pending disaster like a fire or a storm, I can request a ride to a different location or hotel. If I lose my job, I can transfer to a less expensive hotel. If I accept a new job, I can easily move to be near my new employer.

Minimal taxes

I pay no property or vehicle taxes. I also avoid hotel taxes by meeting the state's residency requirement or by spending points for my short-term stays. I can also keep more of my paycheck by living in states with no state income tax, like Texas and Florida.

Free vacations

For most people, traveling means paying a mortgage, utilities, and other expenses while they're also paying travel and hotel costs. I simply grab my bags and move, and my only cost is transportation!

Points and free nights

Loyalty points, promotions, and credit cards help offset the cost of hotel living. I receive at least 20% of my hotel expenses back as points. I can spend points for free nights at any hotel in the same chain. In other words, for every five nights I stay, I receive credit for at least one free night!

Loyalty members can also obtain free nights through milestones and credit cards. For example, my Hilton Honors Surpass American Express card gives me a weekend night award after spending $15K. Free night credits are especially useful for one-night stays, like when I stay at a hotel near an airport before I fly.

Time is money

Hotel living gives back precious time. Because I no longer spend on chores and errands, you can turn that time into a direct financial benefit by having a second job or starting your own business on the side. I decided to write a book!

Cost Comparison

A detailed look at expenses shows that living a carefree life in hotels can be more affordable than owning or renting a home. The estimates below are theoretical but loosely based on my personal experience.

Assumptions:
- Expenses cover two adults
- The individual or couple has a $60,000 combined annual salary. Assuming they pay 25% income tax, their net salary is $45,000 (or $3750/month)

- They pay 100% of hotel expenses personally (They could save money if they occasionally stay with family and friends or if their employer pays part of their hotel costs.)
- Hotel living is $2718/month, based on an average hotel rate of $112, which is $90 after adjusting for the minimum 20% return from loyalty points ($90 x 30.2 days = $2718)
- The hotel rate does not include occupancy tax because hotels reimburse it after meeting the state's residency requirements
- Mortgage is $2500/month
- Rent is $2000/month
- Owning and renting a home includes owning a car
- Hotel living includes using ride-sharing services and complimentary shuttle transportation

		Expenses		
Category	Item	Hotel Guest	Homeowner	Renter
Income	Monthly income, after taxes	$3,750	$3,750	$3,750
Lodging	Hotel Bill / Mortgage / Rent	$2,718	$2,500	$2,000
Utilities	Water	$0	$50	$30
Utilities	Electric and gas	$0	$250	$150
Utilities	Home insurance	$0	$100	$50
Utilities	Cable and internet	$0	$150	$150
Utilities	Community fees	$0	$50	$0
Utilities	Property taxes	$0	$125	$0
Transportation	Car note	$0	$400	$400
Transportation	Car insurance	$0	$75	$75
Transportation	Car gasoline	$0	$100	$100
Transportation	Car maintenance & misc. expenses	$0	$50	$50
Transportation	Transportation	$120	$0	$0
Food	Groceries	$250	$350	$350
Food	Breakfast	$0	$100	$100

Food	Restaurants	$150	$150	$150
Extras	Furniture upgrades and repairs	$0	$175	$150
Extras	Hotel tips	$30	$0	$0
Extras	Household items	$0	$150	$100
Extras	Laundry	$5	$20	$20
Extras	Housekeeping	$0	$150	$100
Extras	Security & alarm services	$0	$50	$10
Extras	Gym membership	$0	$40	$0
Extras	Medical	$30	$30	$30
Extras	Subscriptions, e.g., Amazon, Netflix	$35	$35	$35
Total Monthly Expenses		$3,338	$5,100	$4,050
Net Monthly Savings		$412	-$1,350	-$300

Hotel living has the lowest monthly cost:

Living in Hotels: $3,338

Owning a Home and Car: $5,100

Renting a Home and Owning a Car: $4,050

Following are other significant expenses that make hotel living the most attractive option:

- Gains and losses when purchasing or selling a home
- Costs of initially furnishing a home
- The cost of vacations – the owner/renter pays double rent
- Free hotel nights from loyalty milestones, hotel promotions, and credit card promotions

HOTEL ALTERNATIVES

Vacation rentals are in a larger variety of destinations, and they can be more affordable than nearby hotels. For example, hotel rates in Palm Springs, California are usually upwards of $200/night, plus resort fees, while many local furnished condos and homes charge only $100/night. Renting a vacation home is especially useful when family or friends visit. You can more easily host them when you have an extra bedroom, living room, and kitchen.

Renting a vacation home comes with more chores than hotel living, given the lack of housekeeping and minimal maintenance services. You'll also have to make do without the complimentary breakfast, transportation, club lounge, and business center. Renting a vacation home can also be quite time-consuming and tedious. Different properties using multiple travel portals like HomeAway, Airbnb, Booking.com, TripAdvisor, and Expedia. You can use their filtering capabilities to narrow down options and then review each property's pictures, descriptions, and reviews. After booking, you must fill in paperwork, and read the fine print to help avoid some of the unpleasant surprises.

Hotels offer rates that are refundable up to the day of arrival, but vacation rental bookings are typically non-refundable within weeks of the booking. Even when you find a property with flexible cancellations, you still lose booking fees if you cancel.

Vacation rentals can also come with unexpected distractions, such as maintenance issues, loud, vacationing neighbors, and all-night parties. Hotels are much more standardized—I know what to expect; and if something odd happens, I pick up the phone, and hotel staff resolves the problem quickly if they can. Vacation rentals may include a larger variety of possible unpleasant surprises. I don't necessarily see all the details of the vacation rental I book. For example, there's no indication of whether the master bedroom window is next to a loud highway, or if my next-door neighbor's baby cries all night. I could simply change rooms if I were in a hotel.

I've experienced unpleasant conditions, such as ants in the kitchen, a toilet overflowing at 2 a.m. The day before I was supposed to move into one Airbnb apartment, the homeowner emailed me to let me know the apartment had caught on fire and I needed to find a different place to live. I have also been incredibly misled and then had to fight AirBnB for weeks to finally get reimbursed for a clear breach of contract.

As a matter of fact, I have had to fight to get my money back on numerous occasions. For example, when I booked a month-long stay in Palm Springs through Wyndham Vacation Rentals, I pre-paid for one mid-stay housekeeping service. The contract said the rental company would call me to arrange it. They never called, so in my last week, I called several times, and I emailed several times to request a refund. I escalated it to their management and ultimately received a refund. Situations like that make renting vacation homes more stressful and frustrating than the simplicity of hotel living.

I've also learned the hard way how essential it is to read the contract and fine print thoroughly when booking a vacation rental. For example, I booked a month-long stay through Oranj Palm Vacation Homes, and my invoice included an extra $211 for travel insurance. My subsequent research showed that the travel insurance is basically worthless, so I contacted the company to tell them I didn't want it. It was a bit of a hassle, but they reimbursed the insurance money quickly. Then at the end of the trip, they charged me an extra $28 because I left the key in the rental instead of bringing it to their office. Most vacation rentals allow you to leave the keys in the home when you depart, but I must have missed the fine print on this one.

There are also less expensive hotel alternatives like couch surfing, house sitting, camping, and staying in hostels. They can be less expensive, but they don't have most of the benefits of hotel living, especially when it comes to safety, comfort, and security. Renting an RV can be fun for a while, but it is often unaffordable, comes with a whole new set of chores, and limits international travel.

Living on Cruise Ships vs Hotels

Minimalism and a service-based lifestyle make it easy to cruise regularly. As Satellite Internet services improve, remote working on cruise ships also becomes more feasible. Will my next book be called "Cruise Ship Sweet Home?" Based on my experiences and doing research with frequent cruises, following are the primary differences between living on cruise ships vs. in hotels:

To evaluate the similarities and differences between comparable price ranges, I compare and contract a standard-sized hotel room at a premium hotel vs. a standard-sized cruise ship room:

1. For two people, hotels cost less than cruises.

Hotel living (in hotels like Marriott and Hilton) is less expensive for two people. When factoring in hotel loyalty elite benefits, like points, complimentary upgrades, and free nights, my husband and I can stay in a premium hotel for $100/night, excluding taxes which you don't pay when meeting the state's residency requirement. We can stay in an inside stateroom on a mid-range cruise line like Royal Caribbean to cruise for as low as $140/night ($70/night/person), including taxes. However, cruises provide all my food (plus entertainment), while hotels only include some of my food (e.g., complimentary breakfast). Assuming the free food provides a cost savings of $30/night, premium hotels cost elite members about $10/night less than the least expensive cruises.

2. Hotel rooms are more comfortable.

Premium hotels offer quality beds and bedding. All the cruise ship beds I've slept on are spring mattresses with a slump in them. (On cruise ships, you can request extra bed padding and feather pillows, which helps a bit.) Unlike most hotel rooms, inside staterooms also do not include a refrigerator. Royal Caribbean provided a cooler for my insulin, but there was no ideal place to set it in the tiny room.

3. Hotels offer more flexibility.

I can book hotels as early as the day before my stay. As an elite hotel member, if I don't like my hotel room or I have noisy neighbors, I can easily change floors and rooms. If there's a problem with the hotel, I can depart early with no penalty. Cruises, on the other hand, generally do not offer refunds, especially in the weeks before or during the cruise. Ships are also usually fully booked, or close to it.

4. Hotels provide more upgrades.

As the highest level elite member, I typically receive a complimentary upgrade at Hilton, Marriott, and IHG hotels, often to a suite. Cruise elite members may receive a discount toward a suite, but they generally will not receive complimentary cabin upgrades. The lowest cruise cabin rates are for inside (no view to outside) stateroom cabin, which is quite small.

5. Hotels include reliable Internet connectivity.

Wi-fi is usually free for all hotel loyalty members. Cruise ships, on the other hand, only offer limited days of Wi-Fi for their elite members, otherwise, it is at least $20/day. Cruise Internet service can also be slow and unreliable.

6. It's easy to overeat on a cruise.

Cruises include all-you-can-eat food all day long. Despite my greatest intentions, everyone usually eats much more than they should. You indulge in things you normally wouldn't, such as desserts and fried food. Getting some sun by the pool may encourage you to sneak in a pina colada or a fresh mojito.

7. It's easy to overspend on a cruise.

Port excursions and some of the ship's premium activities (like yoga or a sushi-making class) cost extra money. Alcoholic drinks are also easily accessible and appealing while cruising. It's super convenient to buy anything because you can use your room key to automatically charge anything on the ship.

8. Cruise ships are more social and entertaining.

Cruise ships offer many activities, events, and dining experiences where it is easy to meet and interact with new people. There are also lots of activities and entertaining events available all day every day.

9. Cruise ships are on the water!

Many people find cruising an exhilarating experience. I could stare at the waves for hours, and I especially enjoy the very fresh air. An expensive beach resort can offer a similar experience, but cruise ships also provide an ever-changing landscape.

10. Cruise ships move around!

You can eat or be entertained on a ship without needing to commute anywhere else. You can visit different ports, and you can cruise to a destination in place of flying. One-way cruises, such as Transatlantic repositioning cruises from Florida to Spain or the UK to New York, can also be great alternatives to international flying.

The COVID-19 pandemic affected the cruise industry, and only time will tell how much it will recover. People love cruises so much, many are already cruising through the pandemic – despite the end of buffets and the need to wear masks around the ship.

HOTELS 101

Whether you plan on living in hotels full-time, or want to optimize your vacations, it's helpful to understand your options. There are over 700,000 hotels and resorts around the world. Some cater to business travelers, and others to families and vacationers. Hotels range from simple budget hotels to luxurious retreats. Depending on what you're looking for, there should be a hotel to satisfy your needs.

I usually choose mid-range and premium hotels in major hotel chains to ensure a quality standard. My loyalty to Marriott, Hilton, IHG, and Best Western provides benefits like complimentary nights and room upgrades. Most of my hotel knowledge comes from these hotel chains, and this primer focuses on U.S.-based hotel chains. However, hotel chains around the world, such as Accor Hotels and Jin Jiang International, also have comparable brands and loyalty programs.

Chains and Brands

A hotel chain is a group of hotels that belong to the same company or owner. Examples of U.S.-based hotel chains are:

Best Western	https://www.bestwestern.com
Choice	https://www.choicehotels.com
Drury	https://www.druryhotels.com
Hilton	https://www.hilton.com
Hyatt	https://www.hyatt.com

Intercontinental Hotels Group (IHG)	https://www.ihg.com
Marriott	https://www.marriott.com
Omni	https://www.omnihotels.com
Wyndham	https://www.wyndhamhotels.com

Each chain has a portfolio of brands, which are categories of properties. Following are the five largest U.S.-based global hotel chains, and examples of their brands:

Chain	Brand Examples
Choice	Comfort Inn, Econo Lodge, MainStay Suites, Quality Inn
Hilton	Doubletree by Hilton, Hampton Inn, Hilton, Waldorf Astoria
IHG	Crowne Plaza, Holiday Inn, InterContinental, Staybridge Suites
Marriott	Marriott, Ritz-Carlton, Sheraton, Springhill Suites
Wyndham	Days Inn, La Quinta, Travelodge, Wyndham Grand

Each brand has standards that give prospective guests an idea of what to expect. For example, no matter the location, Hilton's Embassy Suites hotels always offer two-room suites with a kitchenette and living room. IHG's Holiday Inn Express properties offer all guests their standard complimentary breakfast. Doubletree by Hilton offers a free signature chocolate chip cookie.

Following are high-level categories of hotels based on their relative quality and cost:

Hotel Category	Quality	Rate	Amenities and	Hotel Brand

			Services	Examples
Budget or Economy	Low	$	• Private room and bathroom • Toiletries and linens • Daily housekeeping	• Fairfield Inn • Homewood Suites • Econo Lodge
Mid-range or Midscale	Medium	$$	• King-sized beds • Centrally located • Hotel restaurant or café • 24-hour desk	• Courtyard by Marriott • Garden Inn by Hilton • Holiday Inn
Premium or Upscale	High	$$$	• Bathrobes and slippers • Large flat-panel TVs • Suite upgrade possibility • Club lounge possibility	• Marriott • Hilton • Crowne Plaza
Luxury	Very High	$$$$	• Focus on quality and excellent service • Separate bath and shower • Gourmet food options	• Ritz-Carlton • Waldorf Astoria • InterContinental

My taste and my income allow me to stay in mid-range and premium hotels. My preferred hotels are:

- Marriott: Marriott, Renaissance, Sheraton
- Hilton: Hilton, Doubletree by Hilton, Hilton Garden Inn
- IHG: Crowne Plaza, Holiday Inn
- Best Western: Best Western Plus (more often in smaller towns and near nature)

I stick with these properties because:

- They provide a consistently positive experience while also fitting my budget.

- They are consistently safe, have comfortable beds and pillows.
- They have hotels in every country I intend to visit.
- Points, promotions, and special rates make them affordable.
- Loyalty provides complimentary upgrades, access to executive lounges, and other valuable benefits.

Extended-Stay Hotels and Furnished Apartments

Some hotels cater to longer-term guests. Extended-stay hotels, also referred to as apartment hotels or residential hotels, offer suites with equipped kitchens, laundry facilities, and more living space. Hotels like Extended Stay America and Woodspring Suites offer discounted weekly and monthly rates. Hilton, Marriott, and IHG offer the following extended-stay hotels:

- Hilton - Homewood Suites
- Hilton - Home2 Suites
- Marriott - TownePlace Suites
- Marriott - Residence Inn
- Marriott - Element
- IHG - Staybridge Suites
- IHG - Candlewood Suites

Some hotels can provide all the comforts of a traditional home. For example, the Holiday Inn Club Vacations At Desert Club Resort in Las Vegas, Nevada is a refurbished apartment complex with three types of units: one-bedroom suites, one-bedroom deluxe suites, and two-bedroom deluxe suites. All suites include:

- Full kitchen
- Dining table
- Living room
- Two large flat-screen televisions
- Switch-operated gas fireplace
- Separate bedroom with a door
- Large closet with built-in shelves

- Large bathtub
- Laundry room with full-sized washer and dryer
- Balcony

The only downside is that some of the units are available as timeshares, so you have to deal with potential timeshare marketing.

Marriott also offers furnished apartments for temporary housing. Marriott's ExecuStay is a partnership with Oakwood, which offers corporate housing for stays thirty days or longer. Marriott Executive Apartments are available in countries outside the U.S. Both options offer fully furnished apartments with equipped kitchens and a private washer and dryer. Like a premium hotel, lodging usually includes access to a pool, gym, on-site business center, 24-hour security, housekeeping, and concierge services.

Resorts and Boutique Hotels

Resorts supply full-service lodging for vacationers in destinations like beaches, the mountains, and tourist destinations. They cater to people wanting relaxation, recreation, and healing. Rooms often have more space and a kitchen. Resorts offer community activities, like exercise classes and Bingo, and spa services, such as massages and beauty treatments.

Resorts are fun, but resort fees aren't. Resort fees are daily charges in addition to a resort's published room rates. They allegedly cover services and amenities like parking, pool access, pool towels, gym access, boarding pass printing, water bottles, local phone calls, and Internet access. These items are minimum expectations when paying for a premium hotel, especially for guests with elite loyalty status. You must pay for these services, even if you don't use them. Europe and Australia have made it illegal to charge or advertise additional mandatory fees if they were not included in the total price of the hotel when booking.

Only a small number of resorts offer something truly unique or valuable for the resort fee. For example, the resort fee at IHG's

Las Vegas Venetian Resort provides all-you-can-read access to the world's top newspapers and magazines through an app called PressReader. I also take advantage of yoga and other exercise classes.

Five ways to avoid resort fees:

- **Use a corporate rate.** Some resorts waive resort fees for business guests. For example, no resort fees apply when using a corporate rate at Hilton's Tropicana Las Vegas hotel.
- **Pay with points.** Some hotel rewards programs, like Hilton and World of Hyatt, waive resort fees when spending points.
- **Stay at a Hyatt resort as a Globalist.** Members of World of Hyatt's highest elite tier, Globalist, never pay resort fees.
- **Find a resort with no resort fee.** For example, the Marriott Grand Chateau in Las Vegas has no resort fee, even though stays include daily activities like instructor-led yoga, water aerobics, and wine glass painting nights.
- **Talk to the hotel manager.** The advocacy group Kill Resort Fees recommends complaining to the hotel manager about the deceitfulness of resort fees.

I enjoy the Hilton Grand Vacations hotels in Las Vegas because they tend to upgrade me to a spacious one-bedroom suite with a full kitchen, living room, laundry room, and bathroom with a shower and large, jetted tub. Sometimes the nightly prices are low enough so that the resort fee doesn't matter as much. Otherwise, I only spend points to book resorts.

All-inclusive resorts include food and themed activities. All-inclusive resort chains, such as Club Med and Secrets Resorts & Spas, offer themed resorts, such as adults-only, beach spa retreats, and golf retreats. Even big hotel chains, like Hilton and Hyatt, have all-inclusive resorts. However, the rates are per person, which makes them expensive as a couple.

Boutique hotels and resorts are smaller, focus on hospitality, and proactively work to be different than cookie-cutter business hotels. They usually have a quirky or modern theme and offer a gourmet dining experience. Traditionally resorts and boutique hotels are independently owned, but that is changing. Wyndham, Marriott, Hilton, and IHG offer boutique hotels where you can earn and redeem points for your stay. Over 100 boutique hotels around the world are part of Marriott's Autograph Collection. Marriott's Lake Arrowhead Resort and Spa is both a resort and boutique hotel.

Room Types

Most hotel rooms have a single room with one or two beds, an office desk, a TV, a dresser, a closet, and a separate bathroom. Suites are more spacious than regular hotel guest rooms, and they include a living room, dining area, and at least a kitchenette. Junior suites are smaller than suites, and there is no door between the bedroom and the living room area.

Mid-range, premium, and luxury hotels, such as Hilton, Marriott, Sheraton, Ritz-Carlton, and Crowne Plaza, primarily have standard-size hotel rooms, but each hotel has a small percentage of suites. Guests can pay two to four times the rate of a standard guest room, or they can hope for a complimentary upgrade. Some hotels and resorts are 100% suites, including Marriott's Residence Inn, Hilton's Embassy Suites, Hilton's Doubletree Suites, and IHG Club Vacation.

Most premium and luxury hotels have one or more penthouse suites. They are on the top floors and are larger and more luxurious than regular suites. Some hotels also offer Presidential suites, created based on U.S. President Woodrow Wilson's demands during his political trips. His specifications included an ensuite bathroom and walk-in closet, which were both unusual in the 1910s. Suites can also become a Royal suite after royalty has stayed in the suite. The best suites may have more rooms and facilities, such as a full bar and private conference room.

Since my husband and I live and work from our hotel room, a standard-sized room can quickly become cramped. Staying in suites improves our experience because we have more extensive, separate spaces, and we can lounge on a couch instead of our beds.

MAXIMIZING BENEFITS

Most major hotel chains offer a loyalty rewards program. Benefits include complimentary upgrades, free breakfast, and access to club lounges. Members also earn points, which they can use for free nights and guaranteed upgrades.

Following are examples of large hotel rewards programs:

Best Western Rewards	https://www.bestwestern.com/en_US/best-western-rewards.html
Choice Privileges	https://www.choicehotels.com/choice-privileges
Drury Rewards	https://www.druryhotels.com/druryrewards
Hilton Honors	https://www.hilton.com/en/hilton-honors
IHG Rewards Club	https://www.ihg.com/rewardsclub
Marriott Bonvoy	https://www.marriott.com/loyalty.mi
Omni Select Guest	https://www.omnihotels.com/loyalty
World of Hyatt	https://world.hyatt.com/
Wyndham Rewards	https://www.wyndhamhotels.com

Elite Status

HOTEL SWEET HOME

Hotel loyalty programs reward guests for frequent stays. Programs have loyalty status tiers, and hotel stays increase your level. Members receive increasingly valuable rewards as they move up the tiers. New members receive basic benefits, like in-room Wi-Fi and late check-out. Once you stay a certain number of nights (usually ten) in that chain within a year, you have elite status. For example, Best Western Rewards members who stay at least ten nights gain Gold elite status.

Following is a chart of qualified nights needed to obtain elite status in major hotel loyalty programs. Remember to check the hotel rewards websites for the most updated information.

# of Nights	Best Western Rewards	Choice Privileges	Hilton Honors	IHG Rewards Club	Marriott Bonvoy	World of Hyatt	Wyndham Rewards
5							Gold
10	Gold	Gold	Silver	Gold	Silver	Discoverist	
15	Platinum						Platinum
20		Platinum					
25					Gold		
30	Diamond					Explorist	
40		Diamond	Gold	Platinum			Diamond
50	Diamond Select				Platinum		
60			Diamond			Globalist	
75				Spire	Titanium		
100					Ambassador		

Some programs offer alternate qualification options. For example, Hilton Honors members qualify for Silver elite status when they reach ten nights, four stays, or 25,000 base points (~$2500 expenditure). World of Hyatt members achieve Discoverist status when after reaching ten nights, earning 25,000 base points (~$5000 expenditure), or hosting an event three times.

When a rewards member meets the qualification, he obtains that elite status for the rest of the year, plus the following year. For example, staying 75 nights at Marriott properties between January and March 2020 provides Marriott Bonvoy Titanium elite status from March 2020 to December 2021, which means a total of 21 months to enjoy elite benefits like free breakfast, premium Internet, and more points.

Because I live in hotels across multiple chains, I have the highest possible elite statuses across four hotel loyalty programs. My statuses are:

- Best Western Rewards Diamond Select
- Hilton Honors Diamond
- IHG Rewards Club Spire
- Marriott Bonvoy Ambassador

The most challenging status to achieve is Marriott Bonvoy Ambassador; it requires $20K annual spending at Marriott hotels, in addition to 100 qualified nights. Ambassador status offers the same benefits of Titanium, with the bonus of a Marriott representative to personally help me with my stays, as well as the ability to choose the 24 hours of my stay. For example, if my plane arrives at 7 a.m., I can select a check-in time of 7.a.m. and check-out at 7 a.m. the next day.

Status matching

Once you're an elite member of one chain, other rewards programs may match your status. Upon my request, Best Western upgraded my Rewards account from a basic member to Diamond Select status because I have Hilton Honors Diamond status. You can use StatusMatcher.com to help you determine whether a loyalty rewards program will accept an offer for status matching.

Hotels also partner with airlines and car rental companies for status matching. For example, earning Marriott Bonvoy Titanium Elite status provides complimentary United Airlines MileagePlus Silver status. Alternatively, those with United Airlines MileagePlus Gold status can receive complimentary Marriott Bonvoy Gold elite status.

When you reach Marriott Bonvoy Titanium Elite or IHG Spire Elite status, you will receive a complimentary upgrade to Hertz Gold Plus Rewards Five Star. Marriott Bonvoy Ambassador Elite members receive an upgrade to Hertz President's Circle status. The upgraded Hertz loyalty status can help you to skip the lines or receive an upgraded vehicle.

Hilton, Marriott, and Hyatt offer lifetime elite loyalty status, with which you can enjoy the benefits for the rest of your life without having to re-qualify every year, and points never expire. Their loyalty programs grant lifetime membership based on the total number of nights stayed and the total number of years as a loyalty elite member. For example, Marriott offers Lifetime Silver Elite status after 250 lifetime nights + 5 years Elite status. Lifetime Gold Elite status requires 400 lifetime nights + 7 years Gold Elite status. Lifetime Platinum Elite status requires 600 lifetime nights + 10 years Platinum Elite status.

Credit Card fast track

Most hotel-branded programs also offer a credit card that can fast-track a rewards member to a higher status. Cardholders typically receive a middle-tier elite status, like Silver or Gold. Credit cards with the highest annual fee offer the highest loyalty statuses. Hilton Honors allows cardholders to buy their way directly to their highest tier, Diamond. Many of the cards also provide stay credits that help you advance more quickly to the next tier.

For a rapid advancement in loyalty status that won't break the bank, I recommend hotel-branded credit cards that have around a $100 annual fee. You can immediately enjoy elite benefits (if you're not already) while earning bonus points for your stays. From my research and personal experience, I use and recommend the following credit cards:

- Marriott Bonvoy Boundless Visa
- Hilton Honors Surpass American Express
- IHG Rewards Club Premier Mastercard

Following are some of the fast-track offerings:

Credit Card	Annual Fee	Status Fast-track
Best Western Rewards Mastercard	$0	Gold
Best Western Rewards Pre-	$59	Platinum

mium Mastercard		
Hilton Honors American Express	$0	Silver Gold after spending $20K in a year
Hilton Honors Surpass American Express	$95	Gold Diamond after spending $40K in a year
Hilton Honors Aspire American Express	$450	Diamond
IHG Rewards Club Traveler Mastercard	$0	Gold
IHG Rewards Club Premier Mastercard	$89	Platinum
Marriott Bonvoy Boundless Visa	$95	Silver Gold after spending $35K in a year
Marriott Bonvoy Brilliant American Express	$450	Gold Platinum after spending $75K in a year
World of Hyatt Visa	$95	Discoverist
Wyndham Rewards Visa	$0	Gold
Wyndham Rewards Visa	$75	Platinum

Loyalty Rewards

Following are common ways hotel chains reward their loyal guests:

Complimentary food

Many budget and mid-range hotels offer a complimentary breakfast for all guests. Most mid-range, premium, and luxury hotels offer a daily complimentary breakfast to guests with a high enough tier status. For example, guests with at least Marriott Platinum or Hilton Gold status receive daily complimentary breakfast for two at hotels like Marriott, Sheraton, Hilton, Doubletree by Hilton, and Hilton Garden Inn.

Other hotels offer a choice between a food voucher and bonus points. If I am likely to eat the food, then I tend to choose the voucher. For example, some Marriott hotels offer a welcome amenity choice of either 10,000 points or one $10 food credit. I value a Marriott point at $0.075, so 10,000 points are worth $7.50, which is 25% less value than the $10 credit.

Another key to choosing between a voucher and points is to confirm whether the offer is a one-time or daily benefit. For example, many hotels offer a choice between points or free daily breakfast. The daily breakfast choice becomes even more valuable the longer you stay.

During the COVID-19 pandemic, some hotels have eliminated the option of a complimentary breakfast. Points help a little, but hopefully, a reduced hotel rate helps make up for this reduction in service.

Complimentary upgrades

Loyalty rewards programs offer members complimentary upgrades, upon availability, when staying in hotels within their chain. Elite guests can receive upgrades to higher floors, more spacious, deluxe rooms, or rooms with a nice view. Guests with the highest loyalty tier receive the best upgrades. For example, if there are two IHG Elite members, one IHG Gold Elite and IHG Spire, and only one suite upgrade available, the IHG Spire Elite guest will receive it. Only Hilton Honors Diamond Elite members are eligible for suite upgrades at hotels in the Hilton chain.

Lounge access

Some premium and luxury hotels offer a club lounge, or executive lounge, which offers relaxing space with complimentary food and service. Guests with a high status, like Marriott Bonvoy Platinum and Hilton Honors Diamond, receive complimentary access to the lounge. As an IHG Spire member, I enjoy club lounge access at hotels like IHG's Crowne Plaza Amsterdam - South. Their enjoyable lounge includes a massage chair, complimentary food all day, and alcohol in the evening.

Premium Internet

These days most hotels offer Internet access to all guests, although they may require registering for their rewards program. Guests with high enough tier status, like Marriott Bonvoy Platinum and Hilton Honors Diamond, receive complimentary access to a hotel's premium Internet service, which is usually faster and more reliable than the general hotel Internet connection.

Discounted rates

Hotels offer elite members a 5-10% discount off standard rates. I can usually beat the elite rate, so it's my last choice.

Welcome amenity

Many premium hotels give a welcome amenity upon each new check-in. For example, Hilton hotels usually hand the member a bag of bottled water and snacks. Marriott often gives members bonus points as a welcome amenity. I feel most welcome when chocolate or a plate of fresh fruit awaits me in my room!

Miscellaneous rewards

Each hotel chain has a few exclusive rewards as well. For example, Hilton Honors Diamond members can gift another Hilton Honors member elite status. Hotel properties can choose to offer additional perks, such as waived parking fees.

Points multiplier

Rewards members earn base points for hotel stays. Each elite level offers increasingly more bonus points per stay. Members can spend points on free nights, upgrades, and events. You can also combine points and cash to pay discounted room rates.

Extra service

Elite members receive recognition when checking in, and can often receive better service in general. Hotel managers place a priority on making sure their loyal members are satisfied. For example, you're more likely to have success when you request amenities, such as a hotel room fridge.

Earning Points

There are two types of points: base points and bonus points. Rewards program members earn base points for hotel stays. Members earn bonus points through elite bonus points, status milestones, promotions, credit cards, and partners.

Base points

Hotel guests earn base points when paying for eligible hotel purchases, such as the room and food. You cannot earn base points on taxes or tips.

World of Hyatt members receive five base points per $1 spent at their properties. Best Western, Choice, Hilton, IHG, Marriott, and Wyndham offer ten base points per $1 spent at their hotels with the following exceptions:

- 5 points per $1 spent at Hilton's Home2 Suites by Hilton and Tru by Hilton
- 5 points per $1 spent at IHG's Staybridge Suites and Candlewood Suites
- 5 points per $1 spent at Marriott's extended-stay hotels

Staying at those hotels would take twice as long to earn enough points for a free night. For example, a $700 Courtyard by Marriott bill, excluding taxes, earns 700 Marriott Bonvoy loyalty points. A similar bill from a Marriott Residence Inn yields 350 Marriott Bonvoy points.

Bonus points

Members automatically earn elite bonus points on hotel stays. Each elite status tier offers an increasing points multiplier. For example, Hilton Honors Silver members receive 20% bonus points, Gold members receive 80% bonus points, and Diamond members receive 100% bonus points. If a Hilton Honors Gold member spends $100 for a night at the Hilton, he will receive 1,000 points (10 points per $1) plus 800 points (80% Gold elite bonus), for a total of 1,800 points.

Members also earn bonus points by achieving loyalty milestones. Hilton Honors members earn 10,000 bonus points for every ten nights, starting at forty nights. After sixty nights, they receive an additional 30,000 points. This means that after sixty nights, a member will have reached Diamond status and will have earned 60,000 milestone bonus points.

Promotions are crucial to maximizing your bonus points. It's important to always register. For example, Marriott has a recurring "MegaBonus" promotion. To register, I log into the Marriott.com website, view promotions, and click the "Register" button. Now I earn 2,000 bonus points every time I stay at a Marriott hotel during the promotional period. Registering doesn't cost anything except the time it takes to opt-in.

Hotel-branded credit cards offer various promotions too. Credit card bonus sign-up offers can be especially lucrative. Many hotel-branded credit cards offer 30,000 to 100,000 loyalty points after meeting spending criteria. To ensure you receive the sign-on bonus, apply for the card a few weeks before using it for stays at that hotel chain.

Hotel rewards programs offer a variety of other ways to earn bonus points. For example, Marriott guests can earn 500 Marriott Bonvoy bonus points per night when declining housekeeping. Hilton offers bonus points for completing online surveys via their Guest Opinion Rewards website, https://www.guestopinionrewards.com.

HOTEL SWEET HOME

Hotel rewards credit cards also return bonus points. For rapid advancement in loyalty status, hotel-branded credit cards that have around a $100 annual fee offer a great value. I use and recommend the following credit cards to optimize my points:

- Marriott Bonvoy Boundless Visa
- Hilton Honors Surpass American Express
- IHG Rewards Club Premier Mastercard

Credit cards with a higher annual fee yield a higher points multiplier for hotel stays, except for Marriott Bonvoy cards. Following is an overview of the multipliers:

Credit Card	Annual Fee	Multiplier per $1 spent at hotels
Best Western Rewards Mastercard	$0	13x points
Best Western Rewards Premium Mastercard	$59	20x points
Hilton Honors American Express	$0	7x points
Hilton Honors Surpass American Express	$95	12x points
Hilton Honors Aspire American Express	$450	14x points
IHG Rewards Club Traveler Mastercard	$0	5x points
IHG Rewards Club Premier Mastercard	$89	25x points
Marriott Bonvoy Boundless Visa	$95	6x points
Marriott Bonvoy Brilliant American Express	$450	6x points

57

World of Hyatt Visa	$95	9x points
Wyndham Rewards Visa	$0	3x points
Wyndham Rewards Visa	$75	5x points

Members can also earn bonus points through partners. Hilton rewards 3x bonus points per $1 spent on Lyft rides. Marriott rewards 500 bonus points when renting a car through Hertz, and Hyatt rewards 500 bonus points when renting a car through Avis. IHG partners with Budget, Enterprise, and other car rental agencies.

To stay abreast of the latest in hotel and travel news, it's helpful to follow relevant sites and communities, such as:

The Points Guy shares information, tips, and reviews for flights, hotels, lounges, credit cards, and travel gear. Their travel deals and tips are especially helpful for frequent travelers.

Loyalty Lobby is a site dedicated to travel loyalty programs. They have a great newsletter that keeps readers up-to-date on loyalty program changes and promotions. One day I hope to win one of their points giveaways.

Johnny Jet is a site with a rewards and points guide, as well as credit card and travel tips. Johnny Jet is also a contributor to the Travel section in Forbes magazine.

Marriott Insiders is a community of Marriott Bonvoy members who discuss Marriott loyalty status, points, perks, and program policies and changes.

Travelers United is a travel advocacy group. Their work promotes safe and reasonable travel policies, and their articles provide great travel tips.

Spending Points

Unless you're a lifetime Elite member, loyalty points expire.

The only exception is Best Western, where points never expire. With all other programs, loyalty points generally expire after two years of not earning or redeeming points. Because of the COVID-19 pandemic, all of the hotel chains, with the exception of Omni Hotels, have extended this expiration time. However, luck you, at some point, you'll want to choose how to spend your points.

Members can redeem points for free hotel stays, guaranteed room upgrades, shopping discounts, and unique hotel-sponsored events. You could also choose to spend points with the hotel chain's partners. For example, you can redeem Hilton Honors points at Alamo, National, or Enterprise car rental agencies. You can even convert points to a different rewards system. For example, you can exchange 10,000 Hilton Honors points for 1,000 miles with United, Delta, Alaska, or Hawaiian Airlines, or for 1,500 Amtrak Guest Rewards points.

The most lucrative redemption choice is spending points for free hotel nights. One good use is to spend points to stay at hotels that are too expensive when paying with cash but have a reasonable points rate. Spending points also avoids having to pay occupancy taxes, and sometimes resort fees. Both World of Hyatt and Hilton Honors programs waive resort fees when you spend points or use free night vouchers. For example, when I spent points for ten nights at Hilton Hawaiian Village Waikiki Beach Resort, my total bill was $0. I paid no taxes and no resort fees ($45/night!) while enjoying a complimentary upgrade to a suite on the top floor of the Rainbow Tower, overlooking the beach and ocean. Hotel living keeps on giving!

Both Marriott Bonvoy and Hilton Honors offer a fifth free night when redeeming points. Therefore, the ideal way to spend points on hotel stays is to apply them in increments of five nights. For example, a Hilton or Marriott hotel that costs 30,000 points per night costs 120,000 points for a five-night stay (30,000 + 30,000 + 30,000 + 30,000 + 0). The nightly rate of only one night is 30,000 points, but the nightly rate when staying for five nights is 24,000 points (120,000/5).

The IHG Rewards Club Premier Mastercard credit card offers a fourth night free when spending points at IHG hotels, making four nights the ideal redemption period. For example, an IHG hotel that costs 30,000 points per night would cost 90,000 points for a four-night stay (30,000 + 30,000 + 30,000 + 0).

A hotel's points rate varies based on many factors, including the brand and location. Hotels in New York City have a high point redemption rate, while you can spend points at hotels in Atlanta for significantly less. To determine if the rate is a good value, compare both the dollar cost and the points cost of various hotels within a region. If Hotel A's rate is $100 or 20,000 points, and Hotel B's rate is $200 or 30,000 points, Hotel B offers a better value when using points.

Beware of the quality and location of hotels that require a small number of points. A few years ago, I wanted to save money by spending points at hotels in the less expensive country of Panamá. A night at the Hilton Garden Inn Panamá City costs 10,000 points, while an average U.S.-located Hilton Garden Inn rate is 30,000 points. Therefore, I could stay three times longer in Panamá. Since the fifth night is free when paying with points at Hilton hotels, the adjusted points needed is 8,000 points per day. My balance of 500,000 points would allow me to stay for free for two months. It sounded ideal when I booked it.

I learned the hard way that the Hilton Garden Inn Panamá and its nearby sister properties, Doubletree by Hilton Panamá and Hampton Inn Panamá had different quality standards than the same brand hotels in the U.S. and most of Europe. There were roaches, blood on the sheets, mildew in the showers, and filth throughout the hotel. The Hampton Inn Panamá had such strong chemical smells that I couldn't take a deep breath. It's a cautionary tale that you often get what you pay for!

Real-Life Examples

The following examples show how to earn points from elite status, promotions, and credit cards. I receive at least a 20% return on points, so a hotel rate of $120/night costs me $96/night in the long run. I calculate the value of those points as free nights. Both examples are for short-term stays. I benefit from another 7-12% discount when I stay long enough to avoid the occupancy tax.

A Week in an IHG suite

My IHG Spire Elite membership almost always means a complimentary suite upgrade, where I have a separate living room, office area, and kitchenette. Following is an example using my actual IHG hotel bill in Tampa, Florida.

The rate varied throughout the week, but the daily average was $122.51. My total bill for a one-week stay was $960.51.

My IHG Spire Ambassador status and IHG Rewards Club Premier Mastercard provide loyalty points that help offset the costs of staying in IHG hotels. Per the IHG Rewards Club policy, I received points for the room rate and food, but not for taxes or tips. This policy is consistent with the other major hotel chains. My credit card returned 10x points, including hotel restaurants, shops, taxes, and tips.

Following are the calculations for the total points I received for my stay:

Base points = 10 points per $1 spent on room rate:

$122.51 room rate x 10 points x 7 days = 8576 base points

Bonus elite points = additional 100% of base points for Spire elite status:

8576 x 100% = 8576 bonus points

Bonus promotion points = bonus 8,000 points from IHG promotion

Credit card bonus points = 10 points per $1 spent:

960.51×10 points = 9605 bonus points

Total points = base + elite bonus + promotion bonus + credit card bonus:

8576 + 8576 + 8000 + 9605 = 34,757 bonus points

In other words, I earn about 5000 points per night (~35,000/7 nights = 5000).

One night at the same hotel costs 25,000 points. I always book four consecutive nights because my credit card offers the fourth night free when using points. Therefore, the adjusted nightly rate for spending points for a night at this hotel is 18,750 points ((25,000 + 25,000 + 25,000 + 0)/4 = 18,750).

Therefore, for every night I stay, I earn 26% of a free night:

5000 points earned / 18,750 points needed = 26%

My bill was $960.51. After subtracting the value of my earned points (26%), my weekly hotel expenses were $711. That averages to an adjusted rate of $102 per day.

A Hilton night with meals

I stayed one night at the Embassy Suites near the airport in Portland, Maine. I often stay by the airport the night before a flight to minimize stress, and I like Embassy Suites for their spacious two-room suites. My husband and I enjoyed a meal at the hotel restaurant in the evening ($33), and we ate breakfast at the complimentary buffet. The room rate was $124, and my total bill was $177.80.

Per Hilton Honors policy, I received base points for the room rate ($124) and food ($33), but not for taxes or tips. This policy is consistent with the other major hotel chains. My Diamond elite status provides a 100% bonus, and Hilton consistently runs promotions that offer at least another 100% bonus.

I also used my Hilton Honors Ascend American Express credit card to pay my hotel bill. According to the terms, eligible expenses are any costs that "can be charged to your room and paid for with your Hilton Honors American Express Ascend Card at checkout." That includes expenses at restaurants and hotel shops, as well as taxes and tips.

Following are the calculations for the total points I received for my stay:

Base points = 10 points per $1 spent on room and food:

$124 room rate x 10 + $33 food x 10 = 1570 base points

Bonus elite points = 100% of base points for Diamond elite status:

1570 x 100% = 1570 bonus points

Bonus promotion points = 100% of base points from Hilton promotion:

1570 * 100% = 1570 bonus points

Bonus credit card points = 12 points per $1 spent at Hilton hotels:

$177.80 x 12 = 2134 bonus points

Total points = base + elite bonus + promotion bonus + credit card bonus:

1570 + 1570 + 1570 + 2134 = 6844 points

The total Hilton Honors points I earned for a 1-night stay is 6844.

One night at the same hotel costs 60,000 points. That price is not a great value for the $124 rate. Hilton properties usually charge 40,000 points/night. I always book five consecutive nights because the fifth night is free when spending points. Therefore, my adjusted nightly rate at similar hotels is 32,000 points ((40,000 + 40,000 + 40,000 + 40,000 + 0)/5 = 32,000).

My one-night stay earned 21% of a free night:

6844 points earned / 32,000 points needed = 21%

My bill was $177.80. After subtracting the value of my earned points (21%), my one-night stay, including meals, cost $140.

FINDING AND BOOKING YOUR HOTEL

Whether you're looking for a vacation spot or plan on living in a hotel long-term, the first step is to choose your destination. Having a bucket list helps. I would have completed my bucket list already; except I keep adding to it!

After six years of hotel living, I also have well-defined criteria for choosing and booking hotels. I hope you'll find these considerations and tips handy.

Choosing a Destination

Depending on your situation, you may need to select a location due to its proximity to things like your office or doctor. If the destination is a personal choice, you may consider many factors in your decision making:

Friends and family

Hotel living makes visiting friends and family easier if they're spread around. If your budget allows for the transportation, you can visit as often as you'd like and stay until you're done.

My friends and family live all over the world due to my glomad lifestyle. My closest friends live throughout the U.S., Canada, UK, Netherlands, Japan, and Finland. I have also made friends with strangers while traveling. For example, a Canadian friend and I saw a Celine Dion concert in Las Vegas, where we met a couple on their honeymoon from Murcia, Spain. They spoke very little English, and we spoke no Spanish, but we still managed to communicate. We stayed connected through Facebook and mailing each other gifts. Several years later, when I was living in the Netherlands, and my daughter was studying Spanish in school, we took a mother-daughter trip to visit my Spanish friends. They fed us delicious, authentic food, showed us around town and immersed us in their wonderful culture. We had front row seats at a local parade, where we met other welcoming people. It's tough to beat visiting a foreign country with trusted friends to show you around!

Climate

Another benefit of hotel living is that you can move as the weather changes. I prefer a warm climate, and I don't own winter clothes. Therefore, I choose to stay in places like California and Florida most of the year. I visit colder regions like the Netherlands and Canada in the summer.

Time zone

Do you need to consider your co-workers' or family's schedules? Are you a morning person or a night owl? Would jet lag impact your schedule or duration?

My co-workers primarily work on Pacific Time. I am a morning person who naturally wakes up early, so Hawaii's time zone helps make it an ideal location. My workday starts at 6 a.m. and ends at 2 p.m., allowing me to spend every afternoon on the beach. My workday becomes 6 p.m. - 2 a.m. when I visit my daughter in the Netherlands, so I tend to take most of my vacation days when I'm on that side of the world.

Affordability

Within the United States, hotel affordability differs by region and state. The coastal areas are the most expensive, and hotels in the South and mid-West are the least costly. My favorite U.S. affordable destinations are Las Vegas, Denver, and Tampa.

You can travel inexpensively to countries with a lower cost of living, like Thailand and Mexico, but you may sacrifice some safety.

Safety

Following personal safety precautions is paramount for keeping yourself and your belongings safe. For example, I don't wear flashy jewelry or leave my iPhone hanging out of my pocket. I enjoy exploring on my own, but I prefer to prevent risks as much as possible. There are too many stories of women assaulted or killed while vacationing in hotels and resorts around the world. Before I book a hotel or a destination, I make sure they are safe. I avoid areas that are prone to terrorist attacks and violent crime.

You can check the Canada Travel Advisory, U.S. Department of State Website, or sign up for U.S. Travel Advisory notifications. You may also want to search the Internet to see if your desired destination has been in the news.

Language

Choosing English-speaking destinations can help minimize any stress and risk associated with getting around without knowing the language. Translation technology is continually getting better, but it's still easier to chat without barriers.

Following are countries where English is the official, primary language:

- Australia
- Belize
- Canada
- Cook Islands
- Ghana
- Grenada
- Guyana
- Ireland
- Kenya
- Liberia

- New Zealand
- Nigeria
- Philippines
- Sierra Leone
- Singapore
- South Africa
- United Kingdom (England, Scotland, Wales, and Northern Ireland)
- United States

If you're looking for relaxation and fun on a beach, the Caribbean Islands include a plethora of English-speaking destinations:

- Anguilla
- Antigua and Barbuda
- The Bahamas
- Barbados
- British Virgin Islands
- Cayman Islands
- Dominica
- Jamaica
- Montserrat
- Saint Kitts and Nevis
- Saint Lucia
- Sint Maarten
- Saint Vincent and the Grenadines
- Trinidad and Tobago
- Turks and Caicos Islands
- U.S. Virgin Islands

Traveling to English-speaking territories may be more comfortable, but consider visiting countries with unique and interesting cultures, like Japan, India, Korea, or Egypt. By staying at global hotel brands, hotel staff often speak English and can help you. Best of all, exposure to a variety of cultures is life-enriching. I have learned a tremendous amount through my travels around Europe, North America, and Central America.

I once took a month-long lone European vacation, starting with a cheap flight to Katowice, Poland. Hardly anyone spoke English, and handy translation apps didn't exist back then. I had loads of fun using hand gestures and laughing with strangers while we tried to communicate with each other. At one point, I became confused about how to access my train. I asked a Polish police officer if he spoke English, and I was happy he responded with yes. He kindly answered my questions and guided me. This experience gave me greater confidence and a desire for international travel.

Attractions and tourist destinations

You may be interested in a variety of attractions, like a beautiful sunset, a park, a mall, or a Michelin-star restaurant. You may want to drink champagne at the Eiffel Tower (worth it!) or visit Niagara Falls (too crowded for my taste).

I'm a sucker for amusement parks. I have visited several parks around the world, and none can come close to the charm of the Efteling in the Netherlands. It is both a nature and an amusement park. There are beautiful flowers and animals to enjoy while taking a leisurely boat or giant snail ride. The park has a variety of fun rides for people of all ages. Since my daughter lives in the Netherlands, I enjoy making the Efteling a regular fun excursion when I visit.

I also enjoy casinos, which is why I lived at the Monte Carlo casino (now called The Park MGM) in Las Vegas for two months. I gambled every single day. My budget was only $10/day, but that's all I needed to have a great time and even win money. I know the odds are supposed to be random, but I'm a believer in "winning machines." Because I stayed so long, I identified the quarter machines that seem to hit the most, like a couple of Ghostbusters and Michael Jackson slots. I stored my winnings at the end of each day, and at the end of my trip, I had more than I started with. I also entered a free slots tournament and won a bonus $500! Living in a casino was a super fun and easy way to make money.

People often ask me if I've been to Rome, Italy when they meet me and see my last name (Rome). I am happy to say yes! Rome had been on my bucket list for a long time before I learned to truly appreciate its food, wine, and culture. Visiting the local attractions, like the Colleseum, Trevi Fountain, and the Pantheon, is like being in ancient times, or in a classic movie. The rich history, beautiful art, and interesting architecture of Vatican City's Sistine Chapel's also moved me. Sometimes tourist destinations are worth every effort and penny.

City vs. nature

Most hotels are near major highways, airports, city centers, and tourist spots, rather than near nature. Their location offers convenience, but occasional access to nature is good for the soul. You can find budget hotels like Best Western and Holiday Inn Express in smaller towns, which can offer a nice reprieve from living in the city. For example, I enjoyed nature and sightseeing at the Best Western Plus Nanaimo on Vancouver Island, Canada.

Choosing a Hotel

Once you've chosen your destination, you can use a map to narrow down the areas you'd like to be near. There are several factors to ensure your hotel will meet your needs. One consideration is the hotel brand. Lodgings and service offerings differ by hotel brands. Budget hotels like Best Western offer a basic room, while Embassy Suites have a separate living room and kitchenette. Hampton Inn provides a basic free breakfast for all guests, while Hilton hotels offer a more upscale breakfast buffet that is free only to elite guests of a certain level.

It's helpful to read former guest reviews via sites like Google Maps and TripAdvisor. I read a hotel's most recent reviews and worst reviews to get an idea of what to expect. You can also check hotel reviews on my travel blog. For example, I reviewed seven Hilton-branded hotels via my Hiltons of London post.

Keep in mind that guests who review budget hotels have

different expectations than those who review luxury hotels. For example, don't necessarily believe the feedback of a "great breakfast!" review for a Holiday Inn Express. In my experience, their breakfast is always the same - tasteless eggs, instant oatmeal, and fruit that's too ripe to eat.

Other considerations may apply:

- Desirable nearby restaurants, shops, offices, and attractions
- Undesirable, loud nearby facilities, like hospitals, parking garages, and bars
- Pet policy, if you have a pet
- Smoking policy, if you smoke
- Parking fees, if you have a car
- Resort fees

Of course, you'll also want to make sure you get a good rate.

Getting the Best Rate

Depending on your budget and your destination's hotel options, you may choose a budget hotel, a luxury hotel, or somewhere in between. Ensuring you're getting the best value for your money requires a bit of research.

Travel portals, such as Booking.com, Expedia, and TripAdvisor, can offer lower rates than what the hotel directly provides. However, hotel rewards benefits will not apply. For example, your stay will not be eligible for points nor free Wi-Fi. Hotels offer priority services to guests who book directly. For instance, if anything goes wrong during your stay, you're more likely to get a refund when you've booked directly. Another reason for booking direct rather than through these travel portals is because of the often inflexible, non-refundable rates and the risky fine print. I only use hotel websites and apps to compare prices.

Some research and analysis can ensure you're getting the best rate:

- **Are you getting a good value compared to other hotels?**
- **Does the hotel rate start with "From"?** Some hotels, like IHG, often display only the least expensive night during your stay. Be sure to click Rate Details to see the daily breakdown.
- **Does the rate change on the weekends?** To minimize the increased costs, consider checking in on a Monday and checking out on a Friday.
- **Does the rate change if you book different dates?** Could there be a local convention or other events that are causing the rate to be higher than average?
- **Could you get a better price if you change your duration?** For example, some hotels offer a long-term rate if you stay longer than two weeks. In other cases, you can get the best price by breaking down long-term stays into shorter ones.

Following are additional ways to get the lowest rate:

Book at affordable hotels

The average cost of hotels varies by region. The mid-western and southern parts of the United States offer more affordable rates than either coast. For example, I can book premium hotels in Tampa, Florida, between $90 and $130 per night. The same hotel brands are available in Los Angeles, California for $150 to $300. You can also enjoy affordable luxury hotels in some countries outside the U.S., like Panamá and Thailand. I enjoyed a luxurious experience at the Waldorf Astoria in Panamá for under $130/night.

The location of the hotel within the city also affects the price. Usually, the most expensive hotels are downtown or near a tourist attraction, and the least costly are by airports. Tampa, Florida's airport is in a lovely location called Westshore, so the nearby hotels are both affordable and upscale.

Stay off-peak

Hotels in tourist destinations may have periods where they charge a higher rate when the demand is higher. For example, a summer night at the Holiday Inn in Portland, Maine, costs over $280, but their average standard rate for the remainder of the year is $160. Hotels also offer promotions that make them more affordable during off-peak times. These rates are usually non-refundable, so I only book them when my plans are solid.

Use a discount code

Corporate, government, senior, and AAA rates are usually the most discounted rates. They also typically have no penalty for cancellations up to 6 p.m. on the day of check-in.

Large companies have a partnership with the major hotel chains, and their members enjoy deeply discounted rates. For example, major corporations like Accenture negotiate corporate rates with hotel chains like Hilton for a deeply discounted rate for employees' use. If you work for one of those companies, you can find the relevant hotel corporate codes at HotelCorporateCodes.com.

You could also join organizations that have negotiated corporate rates with hotel chains. As a leader of an organization, I could register with corporate lodging networks like CLC Lodging, which provides discounted hotel rates for its members. Even sports organizations like the Northern California Golf Organization (NCGO) have discount codes.

Veterans and seniors can also get discounts. Marriott's Senior rate is for guests at least 62 years old and must be 65 to be eligible for Hilton's Senior rate. I am not eligible for those rates yet, but I do leverage Best Western's and Hilton's AARP (American Association of Retired Persons) discounted rates. You can get an AARP membership when you or your spouse is over the age of 50.

Leverage promotions

Hotels and credit cards also have various promotions where they offer rate discounts, especially during off-peak times. I have used these promotional rates to stay in the best hotels around the world. These rates are typically non-refundable, so I only book them when my plans are solid.

The key to benefitting from a promotion is to register for it. Be sure to sign up for loyalty rewards e-mail notifications and check the hotel and credit card website regularly.

Book in advance

The more advance notice you can give, the better the rates can sometimes be. Be aware that the lowest rates are often non-refundable.

Request a long-term rate

I have had success negotiating a long-term rate by talking with the hotel manager on the phone before my stay. In other cases, I stayed for a while before negotiating a better long-term price. For example, after enjoying a room at the Doubletree by Hilton Hotel Alana – Waikiki Beach, Hawaii, I asked for a meeting with the hotel manager. I explained my situation and that I'd love to stay for a while. He arranged a long-term rate and upgraded my room to a junior suite.

Booking Tips

Each hotel chain allows members to maintain a profile where they can add their default credit card, specify discount codes, and define their room preferences, such as a King or two double beds, and a high or low floor. Members can also request default amenities in their room. For example, when I arrive at a new Marriott hotel, my room includes extra feather pillows and a refrigerator because I requested them in my Bonvoy profile. Once you've set up your profile, booking a hotel can take less than a minute. However, you must be diligent not to make mistakes. Over the years, I've learned to take the following precautions when booking:

- **Confirm you're on the correct website**. When searching

the Internet for a hotel, the top search results may be to other sites. Make sure the URL domain name (the part after www) is the hotel chain name, and not sites like besthoteloffers.com, booking.com, home2go.com, hotels.com, expedia.com, reservationcounter.com, reservationdesk.com, or travelocity.com.

- **Read the cancellation policy.** Is the rate refundable if your plans change? How much notice must you give?
- **Confirm the rates.** Read the rate details to ensure there are no surprises.
- **Confirm the dates.** Does the check-in date match the check-out date of your previous reservation?
- **Confirm the street address.** Are you booking the hotel you think you are? Sometimes there are multiple hotels with the same or similar names in the same geographic location. For example, I meant to book a stay at the Marriott Residence Inn in Old Town Pasadena, California. I accidentally booked "Residence Inn Pasadena Arcadia," which is in a nearby town, not actually in Pasadena.
- **Request any extras.** Unless it's already in my hotel profile, I add the following request to the Requests/Comments section of the booking: "Refrigerator, microwave, robes, slippers, and an extra towel set, please." These items are already in my room when I arrive.

As soon as I book a hotel, I can add it to my iPhone calendar. Seeing the booking in my schedule offers a final way to make sure the booking dates are correct. The sooner I see a mistake, the better chances I have of correcting it by calling the hotel.

If all else fails, hotel loyalty and being nice can help minimize costly mistakes. For example, I have occasionally checked into a hotel and discovered I had accidentally booked multiple overlapping or simultaneous stays. When that happens, I apologize for my mistake and ask if I could avoid cancellation fees or other penalties.

OPTIMIZING YOUR STAY

When I check into a new hotel, I'm usually there to stay for weeks or months, rather than just days. Therefore, it's essential to make sure everything is in order before I settle into my room. After hundreds of stays in a variety of hotels around the world, I have developed some tips that keep hotel living as stress-free as possible.

The checklists help ensure that my hotel experience will meet my needs, like having a refrigerator for my insulin and food or getting a good night's sleep. They also help me get my preferences, such as complimentary suite upgrades.

Check-In and Check-Out Checklists

When I check into a hotel, I use the hotel app or work with the front desk to identify the best room given my preferences. I am a light sleeper, so I prefer to be on a high floor, away from elevators. Groups of loud and drunk people have woken me up when I've had a room next to the elevators. I also ask the following questions at check-in:

- **When and where is the complimentary breakfast?** Do I need to show them a ticket, or do I provide my name and room number each morning?
- **Is there a club lounge?** If so, where?
- **Are there guest laundry facilities?** If so, where?
- **Is there an upcoming event or conference for which the hotel is accommodating guests?**
- **What is the hotel occupancy percentage?**

- **Is my room on a high floor, away from the elevators?** Is it quiet? If not, what are my options?
- **Does the room have a minibar?** If so, could you empty it?

When I first walk into my new room, I use a different checklist to ensure the room is functional and meets my criteria. If the hotel cannot address the issues, I request a different room. I check for the following items:

- **Did I receive my requested items from my booking?** ("Refrigerator, microwave, robes, slippers, and an extra towel set, please")
- **Can I hear street noise through the windows?**
- **Are the beds and pillows comfortable?**
- **Is the refrigerator temperature set correctly?** (It's often too cold or too warm, which could quickly ruin food, and in my case, insulin.)
- **Is the safe empty?**
- **Are there enough tissues?** (sometimes housekeeping leaves an almost empty box of tissues, with no backups)
- **Does the air conditioning work, and is it quiet?**
- **Is the room sufficiently clean?**

If I am missing anything or if there are any issues, I use the hotel app or call the front desk with my requests.

When you check out, it's crucial to perform a consistently thorough check to ensure you don't forget anything in the room. Always check every drawer and every space in the room. That includes under the bed, under or behind other furniture, and in the refrigerator. If you still leave something behind, you can contact the hotel with a forwarding address; they will usually forward it free-of-charge.

A Good Night's Sleep

Most premium hotels have thick walls and double-paned windows to help minimize noise. You can also choose a room likely to be quiet; for example, you can request a high floor, away from the elevators. However, you can't necessarily prevent noisy neighbors. If your neighbors are too loud, you have these options:

1. **Do nothing.** Place earplugs in your ears and continue sleeping if you can. The next morning, ask the front desk if the people next to you are leaving soon. If they're not, consider changing rooms.
2. **Call the front desk.** They will send a staff member or security officer to the suspected room and ask them to be quiet. In my experience, this works about half the time.
3. **Knock on the door.** Be willing to join the party. Honestly, I have never chosen this option, and I don't think I ever will because it's too much risk for my taste.

Like many others, I sleep best in complete darkness. I own an eye mask, but I prefer not to wear it every night. I always unplug the alarm clock because of the light, and they are more annoying than useful. I do not particularly appreciate waking up from alarms set by earlier guests. Following are other possible light culprits in hotel rooms and what to do about them:

- **Digital displays, such as a microwave clock and a thermostat** – The hotel often has plastic L-shaped signs perfect for hanging over these devices to cover their screens at night. Alternatively, I use a folded-up piece of paper to cover the display
- **Light from the hallway shining from under the door** – I roll up a towel diagonally and set it across the bottom of the door
- **Curtains won't close all the way** – I use pants hanger clips from the hotel closet to keep it closed shut

Gratuity

Gratuity expectations differ based on the country and region. Tipping hotel staff is not mandatory in the U.S., but it's encouraged. I tip because:

- **It feels good to be generous** – you know the (underpaid) employees work hard
- **It shows your appreciation** – saying "Thank you" is nice but if you can afford a bit extra, tips are nicer
- **Returned favors** – they are more likely to pull some strings if they can

I keep a handy stack of singles. I follow etiquette rules of $1-$2 per bag for a porter and 20% for restaurant staff. Since I live in hotels every day, I tip housekeeping $1 instead of the typical $3-4/day.

Transportation

You don't have to give up your car, but you can. I find driving to be stressful, and I do not enjoy filling my gas tank, finding parking, or maintaining a vehicle. There are too many risks involved, such as getting lost, being involved in a car accident, or having your car break down. Owning a car also means extra expenses like insurance, maintenance, and annual licenses and fees.

Most mid-range, premium, and luxury hotels offer free transportation to and from the airport, and some provide free hotel shuttle service within a few miles of the hotel. Sometimes the hotel keeps a shuttle schedule, but most of the time it's on a first-come, first-served basis. This service varies by individual property, so you'll need to contact them to see what transportation options they offer.

Car sharing services Uber and Lyft are convenient for longer rides and offer significantly better experiences than taxis. For example, Las Vegas taxis consistently have poor drivers and stinky, dangerous vehicles with annoyingly loud TV ads playing during rides. Uber and Lyft have quality standards their drivers and cars must meet. Best of all, ride-sharing services are quite economical, whether compared to a taxi or owning a vehicle.

I sometimes rent a car between cities when the drive is long but short enough to be an enjoyable road trip. For example, I usually rent a car when I travel between Las Vegas and Los Angeles. It's a peaceful, pretty drive mostly down one highway. Status matching has given me elite status at car rental agencies, so I also enjoy upgrades.

I use public transportation to travel around Europe and Canada. I have enjoyed hundreds of train trips throughout Europe – from slow, run-down rides in Poland to the speedy Eurostar between London and Brussels. I use Amtrak trains to get around the United States West and East coasts. I prefer trains over planes because I can walk around, and I can use my laptop and Internet access while commuting. I avoid most other forms of public transportation due to negative experiences. For example, I have been the victim of pickpocketing, and have been hit in the head multiple times in the London Underground.

I typically fly when I travel further than 250 miles. My idea of fun is not going through airport security, lining up for an hour to board a plane, finding space in overhead bins, squeezing into a ridiculously tiny and uncomfortable chair, and dealing with the obligatory kid kicking my seat. My United Airlines Silver status (provided via Marriott partner status matching) helps make the experience a bit better.

Ten Ways to Get a Suite Upgrade

Complimentary room upgrades can mean a higher floor, larger room, or a nicer view. I prefer suite upgrades because I enjoy the extra space and usually a kitchen and balcony.

I tend to receive the best upgrades at IHG hotels. I have received a complimentary suite upgrade at IHG's Crowne Plaza properties on 90% of my stays! Best of all, IHG hotels have upgraded me to a Presidential/penthouse suite multiple times. For example, I booked one night in a standard room at the Kimpton de Witt Hotel in Amsterdam. The front desk handed the key to me with a smile, saying, "We have a very nice surprise for you." I took the elevator to the top floor, to my two-story penthouse suite with a balcony that overlooked the city. You can check out videos from some of my suite upgrades like this one on my Libby Rome YouTube channel.

You can choose to pay for a suite directly, but that can double or triple the room rate. Instead, you can leverage one of the following ten tips to receive a complimentary suite upgrade:

Have a high loyalty elite status

The chance of receiving a complimentary suite upgrade increase based on your loyalty rewards tier. Since I have the highest level, I receive priority over other guests. Some hotel loyalty programs also specify that only certain elite levels are eligible for suite upgrades. For example, Hilton Honors members must be Diamond and Marriott Bonvoy members must be at least Platinum to be eligible for suites.

Book a room with a king-size bed

Most suites include a king-size bed rather than two queen-size or double beds. You're more likely to be automatically upgraded to a suite if your original room booking was for a room with a king-size bed.

Request a suite upgrade before or during check-in

This method typically only applies when the manager is working at the front desk. It also works with any staff at Crowne Plaza hotels. If you've stayed at the hotel before and have the contact information for the hotel manager, it's also helpful to send them a note to express how you're looking forward to your next visit. Friendliness pays.

Book abroad

Hotels outside the United States are more likely to provide complimentary suite upgrades. I am more likely to receive a suite upgrade when I visit Europe or Central America. American business hotels with many repeat customers are less likely to provide upgrades.

Book one or two nights

Hotels don't like to give away their suites long-term just in case a customer is willing to pay for it. However, they readily provide an upgrade short-term. For example, during a one-night layover in NYC, my one-night (Saturday) Crowne Plaza standard room that I booked was upgraded for free to the Presidential suite. It had two bathrooms, a spa jacuzzi bathtub, and a separate living room with board games. I was only missing friends with whom to enjoy it.

Stay off-peak

My best suite upgrades have been during off-peak times. For example, I continually receive a complimentary upgrade to a junior suite at the Hilton Amsterdam during the winter. The same hotel has a high occupancy rate during summers, so suites fill up quickly.

Complain (if deserved)

Hotels may not offer a suite unless there are issues with the standard room. For example, at the Doubletree in downtown Boston, I complained about the loud noise coming from outside the room. The front desk staff upgraded me to a junior suite in a quieter area.

Build rapport with the manager

After building a relationship with the hotel manager, the manager often upgrades my room. For example, when I told the hotel manager of the Doubletree Waikiki in Hawaii that I was planning on staying for several weeks, he assigned me a lovely junior suite.

If I build rapport with the manager, I am much more likely to receive an upgrade when I return as a repeat customer. I'm more eager to return, knowing that a suite is almost guaranteed.

Use Marriott "suite nights"

After staying 50 nights in a year, a Marriott Bonvoy member can choose from a variety of perks, including five free "suite nights." Members can choose five more after staying 75 nights in a year. Last year, I chose this benefit at both milestones, so I received the maximum perk of ten free suite nights. I chose that perk instead of free nights and other options because they are the most valuable to me. They generally expire at the end of the following year. During the COVID-19 pandemic, hotel chains are extending the expiration to two years. Either way, you must be diligent about not letting these perks go to waste.

The Hyatt Rewards program also offers suite upgrade awards. I hope Hilton and IHG learn from them and offer this option as well.

Use a Marriott ambassador

Marriott Bonvoy Ambassador status provides a representative who can support your booking requests. I once told my representative that I was disappointed after a hotel declined my request for suite nights. She called the hotel and arranged for me to get a suite upgrade anyway, without even needing to spend my suite nights.

How to Keep a Suite Upgrade

When I plan on staying at the same hotel for many weeks or months, a suite would be ideal, but the cost is prohibitive. I can't guarantee how long I'll be staying, so I book my stays for a few days at a time.

If I receive a suite upgrade during my first booking, I then generally keep that suite for my remaining week-long bookings. When it's time to check-out and check-in to my next reservation, I tell the front desk, "I have a back-to-back reservation. I am hoping to stay in the same room."

For example, I used this tip to enjoy a Presidential Suite at the Sheraton Agoura Hills for six days. I used a suite night award for an upgrade, and I used a credit card free night perk to stay for free the first night. I then used my loyalty elite points to continue to enjoy that suite for free for five additional days.

EATING IN HOTELS

Eating well while living in hotels can certainly be challenging. Eating out or ordering in from restaurants can be pricey and unhealthy. Room service is a costly indulgence that includes extras fees and tips, which often don't even go to the server. Hotel rooms usually don't have more than a refrigerator and coffee maker. When you grow tired of eating hotel room-friendly food, you book an extended-stay hotel or resort, like the Marriott Residence Inn or the Hilton Homewood Suites so that you can cook your own meals in a kitchen.

Complimentary Food

Complimentary food is helpful since having no kitchen limits options for making your own meals. Most hotels offer a complimentary breakfast buffet, which is either free for all hotel guests or only to guests with a high elite status. Hotels also provide elite guests complimentary food via vouchers or in club lounges. Some hotels serve all guests complimentary food via happy hours.

Hotels provide complimentary water, tea, and coffee. Fresh fruit is plentiful as well. Elite guests or guests who complain may also enjoy treats as gifts from the hotel.

Free food options are limited during the COVID-19 pandemic, but hopefully services will go back to normal soon!

Free breakfast

Many budget and mid-range hotels offer a complimentary breakfast buffet for all hotel guests. Throughout the Americas and Europe, these free buffets usually include eggs, bacon or sausage, cereal, bread and pastries, instant oatmeal, and fresh fruit (usually melon, apples, bananas, and oranges). The Hampton Inn Panamá City offers eggs as well as local items such as fried corn tortillas, yucca, plantains, and a variety of local fruits. Breakfast in the UK includes baked beans. I thought it was strange the first time I ever had baked beans with my eggs and toast, and now it's one of my favorite breakfasts.

Following are hotel brands that provide a daily free breakfast for all guests:

Complimentary Breakfast for ALL HOTEL GUESTS			
Brand	**Hotel**	**Brand**	**Hotel**
Best Western	Best Western	IHG	Even
Best Western	Best Western Plus	IHG	Holiday Inn Express
Best Western	Best Western Premier	IHG	Residence Inn
Choice	Comfort Inn	IHG	Staybridge Suites
Choice	Comfort Suites	La Quinta	La Quinta Inn & Suites
Choice	Econo Lodge	Marriott	Element
Choice	MainStay Suites	Marriott	Fairfield Inn & Suites
Choice	Quality Inn	Marriott	Residence Inn
Choice	Sleep Inn	Marriott	SpringHill Suites
Drury	Drury Inn	Marriott	TownePlace Suites
Drury	Drury Suites	Radisson	Country Inn and Suites
Hilton	Canopy	Wyndham	Baymont Inn & Suites
Hilton	Embassy Suites	Wyndham	Days Inn
Hilton	Hampton Inn	Wyndham	Hawthorn Suites
Hilton	Home2 Suites	Wyndham	Howard Johnson

Hilton	Homewood Suites	Wyndham	Knights Inn
Hyatt	Hyatt House	Wyndham	Microtel
Hyatt	Hyatt Place	Wyndham	Super 8
Hyatt	Zilara and Ziva	Wyndham	Travelodge
		Wyndham	Wingate

The following are hotel brands that include a free breakfast only for certain levels of elite loyalty guests. For example, a minimum of Hilton Gold or Marriott Platinum status will guarantee a complimentary breakfast as a guest of any of these hotels:

Complimentary Breakfast for ELITE GUESTS ONLY			
Brand	**Hotel**	**Brand**	**Hotel**
Hilton	Curio	Marriott	Four Points
Hilton	Doubletree	Marriott	JW Marriott
Hilton	Garden Inn	Marriott	Le Meridien
Hilton	Hilton	Marriott	Marriott
Hilton	Waldorf	Marriott	Renaissance
Hyatt	Andaz	Marriott	Sheraton
Hyatt	Grand Hyatt	Marriott	St. Regis
Hyatt	Hyatt	Marriott	The Luxury Collection
Hyatt	Park Hyatt	Marriott	Tribute Portfolio
Hyatt	Hyatt Regency	Marriott	Westin
Marriott	Aloft	Marriott	W Hotels
Marriott	Autograph Collection	Radisson	Park Inn
Marriott	Courtyard	Radisson	Park Plaza
Marriott	Delta	Radisson	Radisson
		Radisson	Radisson Blu

Most programs, like Marriott Bonvoy and Hilton Honors, offer the elite breakfast benefit to two people. Radisson Rewards elite status only provides free breakfast for one person. IHG Rewards does not offer free breakfast to elite members.

The complimentary buffet for elite guests usually has higher quality food than at the buffets that are free for everyone. For example, Holiday Inn Express serves instant oatmeal, while most mid-range and premium hotels offer steel-cut oatmeal. There are also more options, such as pancakes, salad, yogurt, and berries, and you can often request cook-to-order items, such as omelets and eggs Benedict.

Lounges

Many hotels with a club lounge serve breakfast for elite members only in the lounge. Some hotels, such as the Sheraton Downtown Tampa in Florida, give you a choice of eating in the lounge or their main restaurant. If you want to eat a bigger breakfast in the restaurant and don't automatically get a choice, simply request it. They usually accommodate you, especially during long-term stays.

Some hotels offer elite guests a discounted rate to eat a full breakfast in their restaurant, and sometimes it's worth it. I happily forgo the free lounge breakfast at the Hilton Los Angeles Airport and pay a discounted rate for the delicious international breakfast they serve in their restaurant. I crave their *congee* (Chinese rice pudding).

Lounges typically serve food all day long. They have snacks and drinks during the day and appetizers in the evening. The quality varies from mediocre to gourmet. For example, I didn't need to buy groceries or eat out during my stay at the Doubletree by Hilton London Tower in London, England due to their rotating variety of delicious *canapés* every evening. American lounges tend to serve more fried food.

Happy hour

Some hotels, like Marriott Residence Inn and IHG Kimpton, provide a happy hour for all guests. They encourage their guests to socialize while enjoying complimentary snacks, wine, beer, and cocktails. I find it fun to talk to someone new while enjoying a complimentary gin and tonic at the Embassy Suites by Hilton.

Vouchers

Alternatively, some hotels offer elite guests a daily food voucher to spend at their attached or partner food venues anytime. For example, Courtyard by Marriott properties often give their Platinum and higher elite guests a $10 per person credit that guests can use at their Bistro in the morning or evening. Other hotels, like the Doubletree Mission Valley hotel in San Diego, also provide a daily food voucher in any of its restaurants or cafes at any time of the day, not just breakfast.

Drinks and fruit

Tea and coffee are complimentary in my room. I can refill my water bottle with spring water in the gym. The gym, lobby, lounges, and breakfast buffets also tend to have handy fruit like apples, oranges, and bananas. I leave breakfast buffets with a piece of fruit in my handbag. I refer to it as my daily "purse fruit." I've confirmed with hotel restaurant staff that taking fruit to go is allowed.

Gifts

Some hotels also leave special treats in guest rooms. For example, it's typical for hotel housekeeping in The Netherlands leave a Tony's chocolate bar (my favorite!) in my room. At the Doubletree by Hilton Victoria hotel in London, UK, I once told a hotel staff member how much I love the little boxes of chocolate they leave in my room. The next day, I had a dozen of them waiting for me!

Hotels have given me champagne, chocolate, cookies, cakes,

and fruit platters as apology gifts over the years. Rewards programs also send gifts when I reach elite status milestones. For example, I recently received a quality laptop case and fountain pens for my Marriott Bonvoy loyalty.

Healthy Eating

With some planning and preparation, you could also make healthy meals in your hotel room.

The definition of "healthy" is subjective and personal. What I mean by healthy eating is sticking to eating lots of whole foods, mostly plants, and minimizing highly processed food. Eating healthy while staying in hotels can be challenging because:

- Junk food is ubiquitous and inexpensive.
- Eating or ordering delivery from restaurants is convenient. It's easy to overeat at restaurants because portions are enormous, plus they tend to add unhealthy levels of oil, salt, and sugar.
- Travelling presents a variety of food. It's fun to try the local cuisine and baked goods.
- It's easy to overeat at the complimentary all-you-can-eat buffets.

Moderation and discipline are vital to maintaining a healthy diet. On the other hand, eating healthy in hotels can be easier than in a home because it:

- Minimizes snacking and overeating – there's no pantry to rummage through when I'm bored.
- Encourages eating more raw vegetables and salads – salads are easy to make in hotel rooms.
- Encourages eating more simply – I have grown an appreciation for the taste of real food rather than relying on sauces for flavor.
- Avoids cooking with butter and oil – without a stove or oven, I don't need these high-calorie fats.

I used to own "fat" clothes and "skinny" clothes when my weight fluctuated. Having a small wardrobe demands that I have a consistent body composition. Because I have Type 1 diabetes, I must also pay close attention to what I'm eating. Food with refined sugar spikes my blood sugar and makes it harder for me to control my symptoms. I researched and took online courses to learn about nutrition and what my body needs to sustain itself. As a certified nutritionist, I developed a set of rules to encourage healthy eating practices:

- Don't have junk food in the hotel room (I ask my husband to hide it in his drawer when he buys it)
- Have plenty of fruit and other healthy snacks handy
- Prepare meals in the hotel room rather than eat at restaurants
- Don't watch TV while you eat (to discourage mindless overeating)
- Drink lots of water and herbal tea

I don't always stick to my rules, but an extra walk or hotel gym workout can help make up for the occasional indulgence.

You can carry travel-friendly snacks for when I get the munchies while traveling. The goal is to avoid buying pricey and unhealthy pre-packaged food.

Travel-friendly snacks:

- Apple with peanut butter
- Bouillon or instant soup
- Edamame
- Fresh fruit
- Hummus and pita
- Jerky
- Nuts and seeds
- Orange
- Popcorn
- Protein bars and fruit bars
- Trail mix

- Tuna and crackers

Ordering food for delivery doesn't have to be unhealthy, and it's especially fun and convenient on travel days. You can use services like Uber Eats, but sometimes local food delivery services prevail. One important tip I've learned over years of hotel living is to never order from menus placed under hotel room doors. Those restaurants do not have permission from the hotels, and they often offer low-quality options. Several Las Vegas hotels warned guests that one of the menus was a scam to get credit card numbers. Instead, ask the concierge or hotel staff for recommendations, or read reviews for nearby restaurants via Google Maps or Yelp.

Hotel Room-Friendly Meals

Most hotel rooms do not include a kitchen, but these days they usually have a refrigerator, microwave, and either a coffee maker or water kettle. Major tourist destinations are the stingiest with these items. Most Las Vegas resorts do not offer guests a refrigerator or microwave, nor even a coffee maker or water kettle. However, I usually receive them through my elite status and upgrades. For example, the Tropicana Doubletree by Hilton supplies a fridge, microwave, and a Keurig machine for guests who stay in their suites or dedicated Hilton Honors guest rooms. Other guests must pay a $15 daily fee for a refrigerator.

Some budget hotels may not supply an in-room fridge. The budget-friendly Best Western in Eindhoven, Netherlands, kindly stored my food and medicine in their staff refrigerator.

Just like with my clothes and belongings, I am a food minimalist. I keep my menu simple and basic. On an average day, I wake up and have tea and free breakfast. I usually have a salad for lunch. Dinner rotates between a rotation of my favorite simple, hotel-friendly meals:

- Salad with my raw vegetables (I like to add avocado or

hummus instead of dressing)
- Sandwiches and pitas
- Cereal with milk and raisins
- Granola with milk and berries
- Rolled oats with milk, berries, and nuts
- Chicken salad on a bed of cauliflower rice
- Potato with salsa and chives
- Pre-cooked meat or fish with corn on the cob
- Brown rice (or riced vegetables) with mixed vegetables and soy sauce
- Hummus and pita
- Burritos – flour tortillas with beans, spinach, and salsa
- Tacos – corn tortillas with spinach, refried beans, and salsa
- Soup – e.g., cabbage, bell peppers, carrots, and celery in vegetable broth
- Reheated leftovers from restaurants

Even with no refrigerator or microwave, a hot water kettle enables making the following hotel-friendly meals:

- Oatmeal with nuts and cinnamon
- Couscous or bulgur with raisins and spinach
- Instant soup or noodles

Groceries stores and fast food restaurants have disposable plates, bowls, cups, napkins, and cutlery, or you can borrow more environmentally friendly real eating ware from the hotel restaurant. I carry my own paring knife to cut vegetables and reusable bees wax paper to store leftovers in the fridge. I also own a collapsible, air-tight measuring bowl, which I use to measure and store food, and as a bowl for meals like soup, salads, or oatmeal.

Perhaps the best thing about making hotel room-friendly meals is that there's hardly any clean up required. I tidy up a little, but only housekeeping has the supplies to properly clean.

Groceries

It's fun to visit new grocery stores and choose from an ever-changing variety of items. It's especially interesting to visit grocery stores in other countries. Of course, my meal plans change based on the type of ingredients available. I enjoy the widest variety at giant American grocery stores, like the two-story Whole Foods store in Pasadena, California. I love filling up containers from their vast cold and hot salad bars.

I also use an online delivery app to have groceries delivered to my hotel room. Instacart is an online grocery delivery service available in most cities around the United States. For $9.99/month, you get free unlimited deliveries of groceries, which you order online from local grocery stores. Amazon offers grocery delivery options. Amazon Prime members can pay $14.99/month for unlimited, locally delivered groceries via Amazon Fresh. For no additional cost, Amazon Prime members can get Amazon-branded and Whole Foods groceries delivered in 1-2 hours via Prime Now in select cities.

Following is a handy list of hotel-friendly groceries:

- Fresh vegetables (e.g., broccoli, spinach, cucumbers, radishes)
- Fresh fruit (e.g., pears, bananas, berries, grapes)
- Riced vegetables
- Fresh herbs or chives
- Brown rice, bulgur, or couscous
- Hummus
- Granola or cereal
- Rolled oats
- Bread or pita
- Crackers
- Tortillas
- Salsa
- Beans

- Broth or pre-made soup
- Pre-cooked meat or tuna
- Nuts and seeds
- Raisins
- Chocolate (or a different favorite snack)
- Yogurt
- Milk (e.g., coconut, almond, soy, dairy)

As an example, a recent hotel room-friendly grocery store bill was $70 and provided 21 meals and plenty of snacks for a couple of weeks:

- Hot salad bar: 2 meals
- Cold salad bar with quinoa and hummus: 3 meals
- Burritos with black beans and salsa: 4 meals
- Cereal with almond milk and raisins: 6 meals
- Soup: 6 meals
- Bean chips and salsa
- Carrots and hummus
- Pumpkin seeds
- Chocolate bar

LONG-TERM STAY TIPS

Hotel living offers freedom, flexibility, and fun. However, it also has unique challenges. The system expects everyone to have a home and stay in the same place. Over the years, I have been able to address most of these challenges. The information and tips I've accumulated may be helpful to anyone thinking of staying in hotels for more than a few days.

Occupancy Tax

Hotels collect an occupancy tax, also known as lodging or tourist tax, based on the tax laws set by the region. Some states, like Texas and Florida, don't have an occupancy tax, but state and local sales taxes apply. Either way, hotel tax rates are usually between 7% and 12%.

To avoid paying this tax, stay the minimum number of days required for permanent residency. In most states, that's thirty days. New Jersey has a requirement of ninety days, and Florida requires six months of residence. Most states have a Hotel Occupancy Tax exemption form online you can complete and provide to the hotel. Some hotels have forms, and other hotels reimburse taxes with a simple e-mail request. I prefer to chat with the hotel manager directly.

Another way to avoid paying taxes on your hotel stays is to pay with loyalty points. When you spend points to book your stay, the entire stay is free.

Mail and Deliveries

Sending and receiving mail is usually a matter of visiting the hotel's front desk. Some hotels charge a fee for receiving packages, but you can potentially bypass these fees. I befriend the staff who takes care of the deliveries, and I hang around when I know the packages are due to arrive. If the team can skip the effort of cataloging and storing your parcel, they will usually skip charging you the fee.

I have a post office box at a packing and shipping store in Pasadena, California. I receive a shipment of medical supplies every three months. The store owner contacts me when my supplies come in. If I'm not planning to be in Pasadena, I give him a forwarding address, and he ships my supplies, along with any mail in my box. I can always ask him to forward my mail at any time.

Permanent Address

A post office box will not typically work when seeking official items like a driver's license, bank account, or credit card. Additionally, the government requires a permanent address for taxes.

If you stay in the same hotel long enough, you can use your hotel address as your permanent address. You can ask the hotel manager to write a letter showing that you officially reside at the hotel; this is often a pre-printed form.

The problem with using a hotel address as your official address is that you may not be there long-term. You could miss important mail, like a jury summons. Being lawful is more challenging when you don't fit the mold!

Another option is to use the address of a family member or a trustworthy friend. Make sure you keep a note of all your official addresses. When applying for things like a new job or a bank loan, you may need to pass a security check. It may be impossible to remember the address of every hotel you lived in the past several years. It's easiest to maintain one long-term address, to which your bank account and taxes are tied.

Laundry

When I tell someone new that I live in hotels, one of the most frequently asked questions is, "How do you do your laundry?" First, I own very few clothes, so laundry never piles up. I also employ the following solutions:

- **Hand-wash your clothes.** It's easy and makes them last longer. I wash mine in the shower at the end of every day.
- **Use the guest laundry room.** Many premium hotels, such as Hilton and Marriott, have a guest laundry room with coin-operated washing machines and dryers. Long-term hotels, like the Residence Inn by Marriott, have a large laundry room with several commercial-grade washing machines and dryers. Hilton and IHG Vacation Club suites often include a washer and dryer in the unit.
- **Take your clothes to a dry cleaner.** They launder and fold them, which makes them extra clean and easy to pack. It's nice to show up in a new destination with a clean, fresh set of clothes. I never use the hotel's laundry service because their profit mark-up is too high.

GETTING STARTED WITH HOTEL LIVING

Tired of chores and errands? Interested in a simpler lifestyle with more freedom and flexibility? Do you think hotel living might work well for you? The following steps can ease the process and maximize the benefits:

1. **Choose your destination(s)**.
2. **Choose your hotel chain**. What hotel chains are in your chosen destination(s)? For example, Tampa, Florida, has many Marriott-branded hotels in the most beautiful areas of town; you can find IHG-branded hotels in many small cities. What hotel chains and hotels do you prefer? Chains like Choice Hotels focus on budget options, while Wyndham offers hotels across a variety of categories, including vacation rentals.
3. **Register as a hotel rewards member**.
4. **Apply for a hotel-branded credit card**, which can fast-track you to a high elite status, and you can earn more bonus points to reduce overall hotel expenses.
5. **Choose your hotel**. Within your hotel chain, are you interested in budget, mid-range, premium, or luxury hotels? For example, can you enjoy living at a Holiday Inn Express budget hotel, or would premium hotels like the Hilton and Sheraton better suit you? Which of your preferred hotels is in your chosen destinations?
6. **Gather applicable discount codes**. Are you an employee of the government or a large organization? (Find codes at HotelCorporateCodes.com.) Are you eligible to join

AARP?
7. **Find and register for hotel and credit card promotions**.
8. **Book your first stay** as a registered guest using the credit card.
9. **Ask for a long-term rate.** Build a relationship with the hotel management, then ask for a long-term rate that fits your budget.
10. **Reap the benefits** and earn points toward free stays and upgrades.
11. **Have fun and enjoy life!**

HELPFUL LINKS

Following is a handy collection of websites mentioned throughout this book.

To view hotel chain offerings, register for promotions, and book hotels:

Best Western	https://www.bestwestern.com
Choice	https://www.choicehotels.com
Drury	https://www.druryhotels.com
Hilton	https://www.hilton.com
Hyatt	https://www.hyatt.com
IHG	https://www.ihg.com
Marriott	https://www.marriott.com
Omni	https://www.omnihotels.com
Wyndham	https://www.wyndhamhotels.com

To view the details of loyalty rewards programs:

Best Western Rewards	https://www.bestwestern.com/en_US/best-western-rewards.html
Choice Privileges	https://www.choicehotels.com/choice-privileges
Drury Rewards	https://www.druryhotels.com/druryrewards

HOTEL SWEET HOME

Hilton Honors	https://www.hilton.com/en/hilton-honors
IHG Rewards Club	https://www.ihg.com/rewardsclub
Marriott Bonvoy	https://www.marriott.com/loyalty.mi
Omni Select Guest	https://www.omnihotels.com/loyalty
World of Hyatt	https://world.hyatt.com
Wyndham Rewards	https://www.wyndhamhotels.com

To stay abreast of the latest in hotel and travel news:

Johnny Jet	https://www.johnnyjet.com
Libby's Travel Blog	https://www.libbyrome.com/travel
Loyalty Lobby	https://loyaltylobby.com
Marriott Insiders	https://www.marriottinsiders.com
The Points Guy	https://www.thepointsguy.com
Travelers United	https://www.travelersunited.org

My recommended hotel rewards credit cards:

Hilton Honors Surpass American Express	https://www.americanexpress.com/us/credit-cards/card/hilton-honors-surpass
IHG Rewards Club Premier Mastercard	https://creditcards.chase.com/travel-credit-cards/ihg-rewards-club-premier
Marriott Bonvoy	https://creditcards.chase.com/

101

Boundless Visa	travel-credit-cards/marriott-bofundless

My recommended minimalist-friendly, travel-friendly clothes:

PrAna	https://www.PrAna.com
Tasc Performance	https://www.tascperformance.com

My recommended items that help with healthy eating:

Paring knife	https://amzn.to/2Ks16ED
Bees wax paper	https://amzn.to/2MQevbt
Collapsible measuring bowl	https://amzn.to/2KlIgP7

To book a car ride:

Lyft	https://www.lyft.com Referral Code: HotelSweetHome
Uber	https://www.uber.com Referral Code: elizabethr9044ue

To find corporate hotel codes for discounted rates:

https://www.hotelcorporatecodes.com

To complete surveys for Hilton Honors bonus points:

https://www.guestopinionrewards.com

To check for reports of bed bugs in a hotel (or to report an instance):

https://www.bedbugreports.com

To check out financial expert JL Collins's clever view on owning a home:

https://jlcollinsnh.com/2013/05/29/why-your-house-is-a-terrible-investment

To find local office space where you can work and be more social than working from your hotel room:

| WeWork | https://www.wework.com |
| Co-working Wiki | https://wiki.coworking.org |

To check travel advisories before international travel:

| Canada Travel Advisory | https://travel.gc.ca/travelling/advisories |
| U.S. Travel Advisory | https://travel.state.gov/content/travel/en/international-travel.html |

To order online groceries (in most U.S. cities):

Amazon Fresh	https://www.amazon.com/fresh
Amazon Pantry	https://www.amazon.com/pantry
InstaCart	https://www.instacart.com

To buy and sell used stuff:

eBay	https://www.ebay.com
Craigslist	https://www.craigslist.org
Kijiji (Canada)	https://www.kijiji.ca
Facebook Marketplace	http://www.facebook.com/

	marketplace

To rent sporting equipment:

http://www.lowergear.com

To rent women's clothes:

https://www.renttherunway.com

Did you find the book inspiring, interesting, or helpful? I would be grateful if you could add your review on Amazon.

Follow me on:

Amazon Author Page	https://amazon.com/author/libbyrome
Blog	https://www.libbyrome.com
Facebook	https://www.facebook.com/libbyromeblog
Instagram	https://www.instagram.com/libbyrome
Twitter	http://www.twitter.com/libbyromeblog
Youtube	https://www.youtube.com/libbyrome

910.46 ROM
Rome, Libby
Hotel sweet home

08/24/21

CPSIA information can be obtained
at www.ICGtesting.com
Printed in the USA
LVHW112001080821
694731LV00010B/760

9 781074 431983